CK B-Day 2013
May your 35th year (yikes!)
be filled w/ happiness and
soup. Beastie + Boss
forever.
xx Court

SUNDAY SOUP

Sunday Soup

A Year's Worth of Mouthwatering, Easy-to-Make Recipes

BY BETTY ROSBOTTOM | PHOTOGRAPHS BY CHARLES SCHILLER

CHRONICLE BOOKS

SAN FRANCISCO

Library of Congress Cataloging-in-Publication Data:

Rosbottom, Betty.
  Sunday Soup : A Year's Worth of Mouthwatering, Easy-to-Make Recipes
  / by Betty Rosbottom.
    p. cm.
  ISBN 978-0-8118-6032-1 (alk. paper)
  1. Soups. I. Title.
  TX757.R7875 2008
  641.8'13—dc22

            2007042030

ISBN: 978-0-8118-6032-1

Manufactured in China.

Prop styling by Lynda White
Food styling by Susan Vajaranant
Design and illustrations by Katie Heit

10 9 8

Chronicle Books LLC
680 Second Street
San Francisco, California 94107

www.chroniclebooks.com

Microplane is a registered trademark of Grace Manufacturing, Inc.; McCormick's
spices are a registered trademark of McCormick & Company, Inc.; Swanson broth is a
registered trademark of Campbell Soup Company; Kitchen Basics broth is a registered
trademark of Kitchen Basics Inc.; College Inn broth is a registered trademark of Del
Monte Foods; Pernod liqueur is a registered trademark of Pernod-Ricard; Goya products
are a registered trademark of Goya Food Inc.; Boursin cheeses are a registered trademark
of Unilever; E-Z Roll garlic peeler is a registered trademark of Zak Designs Inc.; Thai
Kitchen products are a registered trademark of Epicurean International Inc.; Tabasco is
a registered trademark of McIlhenny Co.; Whole Foods market is a registered trademark
of Whole Foods Market Services, Inc.; Wild Oats is a registered trademark of Wild Oats
Markets, Inc.; Penzeys spices and stores are registered trademarks of Penzeys Spices.

DEDICATION

To my aunt Betty Mullen, with love, gratitude, and admiration.

ACKNOWLEDGMENTS

Sunday Soup has been a joyous project from beginning to end, in large measure due to the wonderful people who have helped me with it. Mary Francis came on board at the outset and oversaw every facet. She got recipes to testers and worked alongside me in the kitchen. Using her stellar computer skills, she transferred myriad notes into decipherable bytes. I have run out of synonyms for "thank you" to Mary.

Emily Bell has worked with me on six books and once again shared her amazingly creative talents to help develop the recipes for this one. Sheri Lisak, my longtime assistant and tireless worker, never said no even when I begged her to test a recipe over and over again. Ellen Ellis, writer par excellence, helped me fine-tune the text and find my voice. To Barbara Morse, Jane Giat, Deb Brown, and Barbara O'Connor: Bless you for taking time away from your own busy careers to do soup-cooking with me.

Many volunteers tested the recipes in this collection with passion, but with no compensation besides the dishes they created. Their feedback was invaluable. I am indebted most especially to Marilyn Dougherty, Betty Orsega, and Jackie Murrill, and also to Marilyn and Chuck Cozad, Suzanne Goldberg, Cindy Pizzanelli, Tini Sawicki, Joyce Austen, and Ron Parent.

A big hug to my editor, Bill LeBlond, who not only asked me to do another book for Chronicle Books, but also helped me find the perfect subject—soup. Amy Treadwell at Chronicle shared her time and editorial expertise willingly. Thanks to Charles Schiller for the exquisite photographs, to Susan Vajaranant for the gorgeous food styling, and to Katie Heit for the book's fabulous design.

Lisa Ekus, my agent, was excited about this project from its earliest stages and, along with Jane Falla, provided the support that made the proposal a winner.

I would also like to thank my husband, a true soup aficionado, who sampled for supper almost every night an endless stream of chilies, chowders, gumbos, *sopas*, and *zuppe*—even when they were far from their perfected states. And to my family, Mike, Heidi, Edie, and Griffin: Thanks for loving food and never saying no to soup!

TABLE OF CONTENTS

Soup Calendar

Spring
MARCH | APRIL | MAY

Summer
JUNE | JULY | AUGUST

Beautiful Soup! Who cares for fish,
Game or any other dish?
Who would not give all else for two
Pennyworth only of beautiful Soup?

LEWIS CARROLL, *Alice's Adventures in Wonderland*

As a young girl growing up in the deep South, I was surrounded by homemade foods of every sort—platters piled high with fried chicken, fresh vegetables cooked every which way, piping hot cornbread sticks, made-from-scratch cakes, and luscious icebox pies were part of my heritage. But not soup! Perhaps the winter season was just too short to inspire what my mother must have thought of as cold-weather cooking. During the brief January cold spell, she went straight to the cupboard and reached for tins of canned soup. Tomato and cream of mushroom were her tried-and-true favorites. With the single exception of a delicious seafood gumbo that my grandmother routinely prepared, the soups of my youth came from a can.

I was nearly grown before I learned that soup can brim with fresh flavors and that it can be enjoyed in any season. A year in France was a revelation. When I was a junior in college, I went abroad and lived with a wonderful family in Dijon for the first few weeks. My host mother served the main meal, or *dîner*, in the middle of the day; in the evenings, we often had soup with a salad or an omelette and, of course, a crusty baguette. I can still see Madame Paquet in her small but well-equipped kitchen, standing in front of a pot of simmering liquids. Her potages were simple and often made from leftovers, but to this day I purr with delight when I think of the glorious smells that wafted throughout that apartment on soup nights. Later that year, I arrived in Paris to go to the Sorbonne, and was amazed to discover that the humble vegetable soups served in my dorm's restaurant were just as tempting. And so began my love affair with soup. It's been several decades now and my ardor has never waned.

When I first entertained the idea of doing a soup cookbook, I was ecstatic—just the thought of assembling a collection of my best recipes made me smile. This would be more play than work, I reasoned, but how wrong I was! Assembling recipes when you're a full-time professional cook (as I am) is not so hard, but deciding how to organize those recipes so that readers can use them optimally and effortlessly can be a challenge. After toying with multiple approaches, I finally decided that soup-makers everywhere could use a book organized by the seasons of the year. For chilly or cold days, there would be lots of robust fall and winter entries. For warmer weather or on days when the temps are soaring, plenty of light or chilled soups would fill the spring and summer chapters. To make things even easier, I also put together a "Soup Calendar"—a sort of illustrated table of contents—for at-a-glance inspiration. Turn to this handy reference on pages 8 and 9 whenever you need fresh, seasonal ideas for soups to serve.

In my kitchen, I make soups all through the year, and in this collection, you'll find a year's worth of my favorites, perfect for ladling up any day, any season. There are spicy chilies, rich gumbos, blissful bisques, and steaming chowders to counter the cold, plus icy creations like gazpacho and vichyssoise done up with new twists to stave off summer's heat. Inspiration for these soups comes from near and far. Some recipes are deeply rooted in traditional American cooking. Others, like Mama Veli's Pozole (page 77) and Tortilla Soup with Chicken, Lime, and Smoked Chiles (page 47), are influenced by our neighbors south of the border. Still others trace their origins from Europe and Asia.

As a cooking teacher, I have learned that home cooks often need more information than many recipes typically provide, such as detailed explanations of cooking techniques and where to buy unfamiliar ingredients. So in the recipes that follow, I've included "At The Market Notes" with helpful shopping tips, as well as "Cooking Tips" to help make every soup a success. At a glance, you can see how long it takes to make any of these soups from start to finish and what portion of that is prep time. You'll also see whether a soup can be completely or partially prepared ahead.

To help you choose delicious accompaniments, there's a chapter called "Soup-er Sides." There, you'll find recipes for salads and sandwiches to complement the soups in this book. If you're dealing with a hectic schedule, you can choose a 30-minute recipe, such as Spring New Potato and Garlic Soup (page 91). If you have more time to spend in the kitchen, you might want to

try slow-cooking "Melt in Your Mouth" Beef and Barley Soup (page 82) or "Cool Nights" Chili with Chicken, Corn, and Chipotles (page 30). And if you're wondering which types of bread to serve with any of these soups, you'll find plenty of tempting suggestions included with the recipes.

In my book, soup makes a fine meal anytime, but Sunday is when many of us are home with family or friends and have a few extra hours to cook. What better way to start the week than with a pot of homemade soup? Do a little chopping, sautéing, and simmering on Sunday, then ladle up your soup any day of the week.

"When in doubt, serve soup!" is my mantra, and I hope that after sampling the soups in this collection, it will become yours, too.

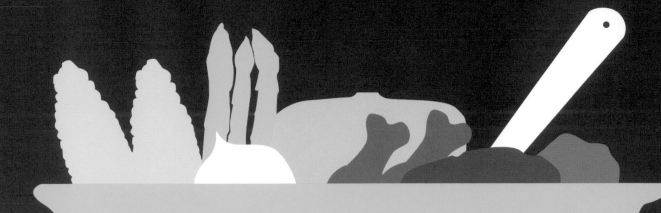

1 "Stocking Up"

SOUP-MAKING BASICS, PLUS TECHNIQUES, HINTS, AND TIPS

When it comes to soups, stocks play a key role. In an ideal culinary world, we would all have stockpots simmering atop the stove with fragrant aromas wafting through the kitchen. But the truth is, few of us today have enough free hours to turn out a batch of homemade stock each time we make a pot of soup. With that in mind, I've organized the stocks in this chapter into three categories: made-from-scratch homemade stocks, shortcut stocks—purchased broths "souped up" with fresh ingredients—and basic store-bought stocks or broths right off the shelf. You can use any of the three stocks interchangeably in all but a few of the following recipes—whichever fits your schedule best. A handful of recipes, notably those for some vegetable soups based on rich chicken or vegetable stocks, should be prepared with homemade or shortcut stocks as noted in their ingredient lists.

Made-from-Scratch Stocks are quick and easy to assemble, but they need slow and steady cooking to develop their flavors. For the homemade chicken stock, plan to spend several minutes prepping the vegetables that season the stock, then allow plenty of time for unattended simmering on the stove. For both the beef and vegetable stocks, you roast the ingredients to deepen their flavors before adding them to a stockpot for slow cooking. A definite bonus: homemade stocks freeze beautifully, so I've included directions for refrigerating and freezing in each recipe.

Shortcut Stocks can be made in a hurry—about 30 minutes. Root vegetables (carrots, onions, and celery) plus fresh herbs are briefly simmered in purchased broths to enhance their flavor. When finished, the vegetables are removed, and the stocks are ready to use.

Store-Bought Stocks are the answer for really busy cooks. Typically, purchased stocks are packaged as broths, although stocks and broths are basically the same—flavorful liquids that result from cooking vegetables with meat, poultry, or fish. These store-bought stocks work well in soup recipes, especially when combined with other flavorful ingredients. I routinely rely on canned chicken and beef broths in my own kitchen.

Made-from-Scratch Chicken Stock

MAKES 8 CUPS

Homemade chicken stock is simple to prepare and one of the best investments of time a cook can make. Although it cooks for several hours, most of that is unattended time while it simmers on the stove. Once finished and cooled, this stock can be frozen for up to three months. It's solid gold in the freezer!

One 3-pound cut-up chicken

2   medium onions, quartered

2   medium carrots, peeled and cut into 1-inch-thick slices

2   medium ribs celery, cut into 1-inch-thick pieces

3   fresh flat-leaf parsley sprigs

1   fresh thyme sprig or ½ teaspoon dried thyme

2   garlic cloves, crushed

1½ teaspoons kosher salt, plus more if needed

1. Combine all ingredients in a large pot and add 3 quarts water. Bring the mixture to a simmer over medium-high heat. Reduce the heat and simmer, uncovered, until the stock has developed a good flavor, for 2½ to 3 hours or longer. Spoon off and discard any foam that rises to the top while the stock is simmering. Add more water if the liquid cooks down below the level of the chicken and vegetables.

2. Remove the pot from the heat, and strain the stock through a large, fine-mesh strainer or sieve. Press down on the vegetables and chicken with a wooden spoon to extract as much liquid as possible. Discard the vegetables, but save the chicken for another use. (It can be used in chicken salad or in chicken potpies, for example.) Refrigerate the stock for 2 hours or until the fat has solidified on top. Remove the fat with a spoon and discard.

3. Taste the stock and season with more salt, if desired. (Stock can be prepared 2 days ahead; keep covered and refrigerated. To freeze, place stock in a freezer container, label with name and date, and store up to 3 months.)

Made-from-Scratch Beef Stock

MAKES 8 CUPS

I've been making this beef stock for more than twenty years—its rich color and intense flavor will enhance any recipe in which it is used. Roasting root vegetables and soup bones (available at the meat counter of your local supermarket or butcher shop) together before simmering these ingredients in water on top of the stove is what gives this stock its rich flavor.

2   pounds lean stew beef, such as chuck, cut into 1- to 2-inch cubes

2   pounds beef soup bones

2   carrots, cut into ½-inch-thick slices

2   large onions, cut into ½-inch-thick slices

2   ribs celery, leaves included, cut into ½-inch-thick slices

1   cup dry white or red wine

2   tablespoons tomato paste

3   sprigs fresh flat-leaf parsley

1   bay leaf, broken in half

1   garlic clove, crushed

½   teaspoon dried thyme

2   teaspoons kosher salt, plus more to taste

1. Arrange an oven rack at center position and preheat oven to 450 degrees F.

2. Put the beef cubes and bones, carrots, onions, and celery in a large roasting pan. Brown them in the oven for about 15 minutes. Watch carefully, and if the vegetables start to burn, remove them.

3. Transfer the beef and vegetables to a large stockpot or deep-sided pot (at least 8-quart capacity). Add the wine, tomato paste, parsley, bay leaf, garlic, thyme, and 2 teaspoons salt. Stir in 4 quarts water. Place the pot over medium heat, and very slowly bring water to a boil. Then, reduce the heat and simmer the stock for 3½ to 4 hours, adding more water if the liquid cooks down below the level of the meat and vegetables. Spoon off and discard any foam that rises to the top while stock is simmering.

4. Remove the pot from the heat and strain the stock through a large, fine-mesh strainer or sieve. Discard the meat, bones, and vegetables. Using a large spoon, skim off and discard any fat from the stock. Or, for an easier way to degrease the stock, refrigerate it for several hours. The fat will solidify on top, and then you can remove it easily with a spoon.

5. Taste the stock and add more salt if desired. (Stock can be prepared 2 days ahead; keep covered and refrigerated. To freeze, place in a freezer container, label with name and date, and store up to 3 months.)

Made-from-Scratch Roasted Vegetable Stock

MAKES 6 CUPS

This stock is fragrant with the flavors of fresh roasted vegetables. I first came upon the idea of roasting the vegetables to bring out their full flavor in Barbara Kafka's cookbooks, and now I am a convert. Once the vegetables are roasted, they are simmered along with fresh and dried herbs.

2   medium onions, halved and cut into 1-inch-thick wedges
2   medium carrots, peeled and cut into 1-inch-thick pieces
2   medium leeks, white and light green parts only, halved and cut into 1-inch pieces
2   ribs celery, cut into 1-inch-thick pieces, leaves reserved
4   plum tomatoes, quartered, membranes and seeds removed
4   ounces mushrooms, halved (or quartered if very large)
6   garlic cloves, peeled and smashed
⅓   cup olive oil
2   teaspoons dried thyme
3   teaspoons kosher salt
5   sprigs fresh flat-leaf parsley
2   bay leaves

1. Preheat oven to 425 degrees F.

2. Place vegetables on a large, rimmed baking sheet and drizzle with olive oil; sprinkle with thyme and 1 teaspoon salt. Roast for 35 minutes. (Some of the vegetables will be quite browned; that's fine.)

3. Transfer vegetables to a large saucepan. Add 8 cups water, the celery leaves, parsley sprigs, bay leaves, and the remaining 2 teaspoons salt. Bring to a boil, then reduce heat and cook at a simmer for 45 minutes.

4. Remove the pot from the heat and strain stock, pressing down firmly on the vegetables to extract as much liquid as possible. (Stock can be prepared 2 days ahead; keep covered and refrigerated. To freeze, place in a freezer container, label with name and date, and store up to 3 months.)

PHOTO OPPOSITE:
Shortcut Chicken Stock (page 20)

Shortcut Chicken or Beef Stock

MAKES 8 CUPS

Pressed for time? About thirty minutes is all you need to turn purchased broth into a full-flavored stock.

- 2 quarts (8 cups) low-sodium chicken or beef broth, plus a little extra if needed
- 2 ribs celery, cut into 1-inch-thick pieces
- 2 medium carrots, peeled and cut into 1-inch-thick pieces
- 2 medium onions, halved and cut into 1-inch-thick slices
- 2 sprigs fresh flat-leaf parsley
- 2 sprigs fresh thyme or ½ teaspoon dried thyme

1. Place 2 quarts stock, the celery, carrots, onions, parsley, and thyme in a large, heavy saucepan or pot (with a lid) set over medium heat. Bring mixture to a simmer, reduce heat, cover, and cook at a simmer for 30 minutes.

2. Remove the pot from the heat and strain the stock through a large, fine-mesh strainer or sieve, pressing down on the vegetables and herbs to extract as much liquid as possible. It should yield 8 cups stock; if not, add enough extra stock or water to make 8 cups. (Stock can be prepared 2 days ahead; keep covered and refrigerated. To freeze, place in a freezer container, label with name and date, and store up to 3 months.)

All About Store-Bought Stocks

When buying prepared broths, you will first need to decide between regular and reduced-sodium varieties. If you will be simmering a soup uncovered for 30 minutes or longer, low-sodium broth is a good choice because the salt in the broth will become more concentrated as the liquids reduce. I also use low-sodium broths when there are other salty ingredients in the soup, such as a lot of celery (which is high in sodium) or fish sauce.

One of the big pluses of purchased broths is their long shelf life. I always keep cans and cartons of broth on hand and I'm a big fan of the quart-size (32-ounce) cartons because they are so practical: You can use just the amount you need for a recipe and reseal them for storage in the refrigerator.

The best way to determine which brands are best is to sample as many as possible, testing them before using in a recipe for taste and appearance. For chicken and beef broths, my short list of favorites includes Swanson, Kitchen Basics, and College Inn. I am less enthusiastic about store-bought vegetable broths, which are often lackluster in taste.

Soup-Making Basics plus Technique Tips and Hints

EQUIPMENT—Soup-making does not require a lot of utensils. Essentials include a soup pot (with a lid), such as a Dutch oven; a stockpot; a fine-mesh strainer or sieve; either a food processor, blender, food mill, or immersion blender for puréeing; and a ladle for serving.

INGREDIENTS—Use the freshest and best ingredients possible. Seasonal produce not only tastes better, but generally costs less, too.

VEGETARIAN OPTIONS—For vegetarian purists, you can replace the chicken stock used in the vegetable soups in this collection with Made-from-Scratch Roasted Vegetable Stock (page 18).

SALTING—The secret to bringing out the flavors in soups is salting correctly. I prefer kosher salt for its clean, clear taste. When salting a soup to be served hot, wait a few minutes for the soup to cool down just a bit before salting; you'll be able to taste the flavors better. Season soups that will be served cold *after* they have chilled; colder foods will seem less-intensely flavored and need a bit more seasoning. And, what if your soup accidentally gets over-salted? Peel a potato and immerse it in the soup for an hour or longer to draw out the salt.

RESCUING TOO-THIN OR TOO-THICK SOUPS—If a soup is too thin, make a thickener by mixing equal amounts of flour and unsalted room temperature butter into a paste; whisk it into a pot of simmering soup in teaspoonfuls to thicken. If a soup is too thick, thin it by adding additional stock or another liquid used in the soup in ¼-cup increments.

HANDLING HOT SOUPS—Be careful when puréeing hot soups in a food processor, blender, or with an immersion blender. Hot soups splatter easily, so use caution and always purée them in small batches.

MAKING SOUPS AHEAD FOR THE FRIDGE OR THE FREEZER—Most soups will improve in flavor when made a day in advance. Let them cool first, then cover and refrigerate. Try not to put hot soup directly into the refrigerator, as the heat may raise the temperature of the items inside, causing them to spoil. When freezing soups, place in a freezer container, seal, and label with name and date.

SERVING STYLE—You can bring a soup to the table in the pot in which it was cooked or make a statement by offering it in a beautiful tureen. For individual servings, use wide or narrow bowls, or ladle soup into cups or mugs. Chilled soups look striking when served in wide-mouthed wine or Martini glasses. And, if you want to be *très chic*, try serving soups (especially smooth puréed ones) as appetizers in espresso or demitasse cups.

A Few Useful Techniques

CLEANING LEEKS

Leeks, with their unique earthy taste, add a robust accent to many of the soups in this book. Since they grow in sandy soil, leeks are often filled with dirt or grit. To clean them, cut off the root ends, then split the leeks lengthwise. Rinse thoroughly under cold running water to remove all particles. Then dry and use as needed. Most of the following recipes call for the white and light green parts of leeks, while the dark green stems are cut off and not used.

PEELING GARLIC CLOVES

Garlic is used extensively in the recipes in this collection. Here's the easiest way I've found to separate and peel them: Wrap a clean kitchen towel around a head and then, with the handle of a chef's knife, firmly but gently hit the head until the cloves are released. To peel individual cloves, lay them flat on a work surface and lightly crush them with the flat side of a knife to loosen the thin paper coating. A new kitchen tool, a small rubber tube called the E-Z-Rol garlic peeler, makes this task even simpler. A clove is put into the rubber tube and rolled back and forth. Because the interior surface of these rolls is made of a sticky substance, the papery coating of a garlic clove is immediately loosened.

SEEDING AND CHOPPING HOT PEPPERS

The tissues around your mouth, nose, and eyes are very sensitive to the oils of hot peppers, so if you touch any of these areas with pepper-coated fingers, you will feel an unpleasant burning sensation! Wearing rubber gloves when seeding and chopping peppers will prevent this problem. Remove the gloves and wash your hands as soon as you are finished.

ZESTING OR REMOVING THE PEEL FROM CITRUS FRUIT
The zest of a citrus fruit is the thin, colored outer layer.
Because this skin contains the oils of the fruit and is packed
with flavor, it makes a great addition to both warm and cold
soups. When grated zest is called for, be careful to remove
only the colored portion of the skin and not the white pith
beneath, which is bitter. You can use a vegetable peeler
or sharp paring knife to remove long ribbons of the skin,
then chop them. Or you can use a citrus zester, a kitchen
tool that you scrape across the fruit to remove fine threads
of peel. But, by far the easiest way is to use a Microplane
grater, a long rectangular metal grater, which is extremely
efficient in removing small bits of the skin without any
white pith.

FRESH VERSUS DRIED HERBS
You can substitute dried herbs for fresh ones in most recipes.
Because dried herbs are more intense in flavor, use one-
third of the fresh amount specified.

MAKING YOUR OWN CRÈME FRAÎCHE
Crème fraîche is a wonderful enrichment for soup and
is available in many supermarkets, often displayed with
specialty cheeses. If you can't find it, the following recipe
works well.

Homemade Crème Fraîche
MAKES ABOUT 1⅓ CUPS

1   cup heavy cream
⅓   cup sour cream

1. Whisk cream and sour cream together in a medium
   nonreactive bowl. Let stand at room temperature until
   thickened, for 6 hours or longer. Cover and refrigerate.
   (Crème fraîche can be stored up to 1 week, covered, in
   the refrigerator.)

2 Fall

SEPTEMBER | OCTOBER | NOVEMBER

I don't have to look at the calendar to know that fall has arrived in my small New England town: The golden, orange, and russet leaves announce that a new season is under way. Days gradually become shorter, temperatures start to dip, and autumn harvests begin to make an appearance at the market. At these first signs, I know it's time to pull out my stockpot. Autumn is prime time for soup-makers. Is there anything more satisfying on a crisp, cool day than a bowl of homemade soup?

The soups in this chapter reflect the bounty of the fall market. Apples, pears, pumpkins, and even some carryover crops from late summer find their way into these recipes. With the last of the year's corn, you can make a delectable Scallop and Corn Chowder. Later on in the season, try Apple Soup with Crumbled Roquefort and Bacon, indulge in Creamy Stilton Soup with Sautéed Pears, or sample Butternut Squash and Apple Soup with Cider Cream.

Fortunately, fall brings with it many opportunities to share. Autumn picnics and tailgates are much more festive when a thermos of hot soup is on the menu. Fabulous Fall Roots Soup—an orange-hued autumnal purée—or White Cheddar Creams with Crispy Bacon would make great additions to such occasions. And on Thanksgiving, the most important food holiday of the year, why not begin your feast with Sweet Potato Soup with Orange Crème Fraîche or Pumpkin Soup with Toasted Walnuts and Rosemary. Happily for the cook, both of these soups (like many in this collection) can be prepared well in advance.

There are many things I love about fall—bundling up again in a favorite sweater, building a crackling fire, or even raking the leaves (for the first time, anyway). But the thing I love best, setting a pot of hearty soup to simmer on the stove, makes me savor all the season's pleasures that much more.

Butternut Squash and Apple Soup with Cider Cream

In New England, where I live, two of the most prolific fall crops are apples and squashes. Inspired by these two seasonal treasures, I combined Granny Smith apples with butternut squash to create the recipe that follows. A swirl of cider cream (made with cider that has been reduced, then combined with sour cream) and crispy bits of bacon top this silken-smooth mixture that delectably combines sweet, tart, and salty flavors.

SERVINGS: 6

PREP TIME:
20 to 30 minutes

START TO FINISH:
1 hour 20 minutes

MAKE AHEAD:
Yes

BREAD BASKET CHOICE:
Crusty baguette or whole wheat loaf

SOUP-ER SIDE:
Best-Ever Greens Salad in Classic Vinaigrette (page 139), or omit bread and serve Turkey Panini with White Cheddar and Cranberry Chutney (page 157)

---

5   tablespoons unsalted butter

6   cups peeled, seeded, and cubed butternut squash (from 2- to 2½-pound squash; cut into ½-inch cubes; see note and tip on page 28)

2   cups chopped leeks, white and light green parts only (about 3 medium leeks)

½   cup coarsely chopped carrots

½   cup coarsely chopped celery

2   small Granny Smith apples, peeled, cored, and chopped, plus an extra apple for garnish

1½ teaspoons dried thyme

½   teaspoon crumbled dried sage

5   cups chicken stock

1½ cups apple cider, divided

Kosher salt

⅔   cup sour cream

5   bacon slices, sautéed until crisp, drained, and crumbled

---

1. Melt the butter in a large, heavy pan set over medium-high heat. When hot, add squash, leeks, carrots, and celery and sauté, stirring frequently, until vegetables have softened slightly, 10 to 12 minutes. Add apples, thyme, and sage. Add stock and 1 cup of the cider. Bring mixture to a simmer. Reduce heat, cover, and simmer gently until vegetables and apples are tender, stirring occasionally, for about 30 minutes. Remove from heat and cool slightly.

2. Meanwhile, make the cider cream. Boil remaining ½ cup cider in a small, heavy saucepan until it reduces to ¼ cup, for about 5 minutes. Cool, then place sour cream in a small bowl and whisk in reduced cider. (Cider cream can be prepared 1 day ahead; cover and refrigerate until needed.)

3. Purée the soup in batches in a food processor, blender, or food mill, and return soup to the pot. (Or use an immersion blender to purée the soup in the pot.) Taste soup and season with salt, as needed. (Soup can be prepared 1 day ahead. Cool, cover, and refrigerate. Reheat over medium heat.)

continued on next page…

...continued

4. For the garnish, halve and core the reserved apple, then cut one half into 12 paper-thin slices. (Eat or save remaining half for another use.)

5. To serve, ladle soup into 6 shallow bowls and drizzle with cider cream. Garnish each serving with crumbled bacon and a couple of apple slices.

 AT THE MARKET NOTE:

Butternut squash can be purchased already peeled and cut into chunks at many supermarkets—a big time-saver.

 COOKING TIP:

To peel hard squashes, halve them lengthwise and scoop out the seeds with a spoon. Then, using a sharp knife or vegetable peeler, remove the skin in strips.

Creamy Stilton Soup with Sautéed Pears

Pears and Stilton (England's famous blue-veined cheese) are always a winning combination. In this rich, smooth soup, crumbled Stilton is whisked into a puréed potato-and-vegetable mixture, adding a distinctive, slightly salty note that is a delicious foil for the garnish of sweet, golden sautéed pear slices.

SERVINGS: 6

PREP TIME:
20 minutes

START TO FINISH:
1 hour

MAKE AHEAD:
Partially

BREAD BASKET
CHOICE:
Crusty baguette or
sourdough loaf

SOUP-ER SIDE:
Best-Ever Greens Salad
in Classic Vinaigrette
(page 139), made with
baby spinach

5	tablespoons unsalted butter
2	cups chopped leeks, white and light green parts only (about 3 medium leeks)
1	cup coarsely chopped celery
2	pounds (about 4 medium) red-skin or Yukon gold potatoes, peeled and cut into ½-inch cubes
6	cups chicken stock
½	teaspoon crushed dried rosemary (see note), or 1 ½ teaspoons chopped fresh rosemary
10	ounces crumbled Stilton or other blue cheese
½	cup half-and-half
	Kosher salt

GARNISH

2	Bartlett pears, ripe but not too soft
2	tablespoons unsalted butter
½	teaspoon sugar
¼	teaspoon crushed dried rosemary or ¾ teaspoon chopped fresh rosemary
	Fresh rosemary sprigs for garnish

 AT THE MARKET NOTE:

To save time, buy crushed dried rosemary, rather than whole dried rosemary leaves that you must crush yourself. Crushed dried rosemary can be found in the spice section of most supermarkets. McCormick's brand is widely available.

1. Heat butter in a large, heavy pot set over medium heat. When hot, add the leeks and celery and sauté, stirring, until softened, about 5 minutes. Add the cubed potatoes, stock, and dried or fresh rosemary. Bring to a simmer, then reduce heat and simmer uncovered until vegetables are very tender, for 20 to 25 minutes.

2. Purée the soup in batches in a food processor, blender, or food mill, and return soup to the pot. (Or use an immersion blender to purée the soup in the pot.) Set the pot over low heat. Whisk in the cheese until it melts. Whisk in the half-and-half and cook 1 minute more. Taste soup and season with salt, as needed. (Soup can be prepared 1 day ahead. Cool, cover, and refrigerate. Reheat over low heat.)

3. To make the pear garnish, peel, core, and halve the pears lengthwise. Cut each half into ½-inch-thick slices. In a medium skillet, heat the butter over medium heat. When hot, add the pear slices and cook until golden brown on the underside, for 3 to 4 minutes. Sprinkle with a little sugar. Turn and cook until golden brown on the other side, for 2 to 3 minutes more. Sprinkle with dried or fresh rosemary.

4. To serve, ladle the soup into 6 bowls and garnish each serving with 2 to 3 pear slices and a rosemary sprig.

"Cool Nights" Chili with Chicken, Corn, and Chipotles

When fall arrives, I love to make this special chili. A pot of the spicy broth simmering on the stove, with its piquant aromas scenting the kitchen, takes the chill off blustery days and cool nights. In this version, I replace the traditional ground beef with diced chicken breast and add fresh corn kernels along with the regulation beans. Chili powder provides that familiar spicy accent, while chopped chipotle peppers add a layer of smoky heat. Piping hot bowls of the chili are garnished with dollops of sour cream and a sprinkling of chopped cilantro.

SERVINGS: 6

PREP TIME:
30 minutes

START TO FINISH:
1 hour 15 minutes

MAKE AHEAD:
Yes

BREAD BASKET
CHOICE:
Cornbread or
tortilla chips

SOUP-ER SIDE:
Red, Yellow, and
Orange Pepper Salad
with Tequila-Lime
Dressing (page 148)

5 ½ tablespoons canola or vegetable oil, divided

1 ½ pounds boneless, skinless chicken breasts, cut into ½-inch cubes

2 cups chopped onions

¼ cup all-purpose flour

2 tablespoons chili powder

1 tablespoon ground cumin

1 teaspoon salt, plus more if needed

4 cups chicken stock

One 28-ounce can Italian-style tomatoes, drained and coarsely chopped

3 canned chipotle peppers in adobo sauce, coarsely chopped

3 ½ to 4 cups fresh corn kernels (4 to 5 ears of corn) or frozen corn kernels, thawed

Two 19-ounce cans dark kidney beans, rinsed and drained

GARNISH

½ cup sour cream

2 tablespoons chopped cilantro (optional)

1 large lime, cut into 6 wedges

1. Heat 4 tablespoons oil in a large, deep-sided pot (with a lid) set over medium-high heat. When hot, add the chicken and sauté until light golden, for 4 to 5 minutes. Remove chicken from pan and drain on paper towels. Add remaining 1 ½ tablespoons oil to the pan. When oil is very hot, add onions and cook, stirring, until lightly browned, for 3 to 4 minutes. Return sautéed chicken to the pan.

2. Stir together flour, chili powder, cumin, and 1 teaspoon salt in a small bowl. Sprinkle the mixture over the onions and chicken, and cook, stirring, 1 minute more. Add stock, tomatoes, and chipotles; bring mixture to a simmer. Reduce heat, cover, and cook until chicken is fork-tender and mixture has thickened slightly, for 25 to 30 minutes.

3. Add corn and beans, and cook for 10 minutes more. Taste chili and season with salt, if needed. (Chili can be prepared 2 days ahead. Cool, cover, and refrigerate. Reheat, uncovered, over medium heat.)

4. To serve, ladle chili into bowls. Garnish each serving with a generous dollop of sour cream and a sprinkling of chopped cilantro, if desired. Serve each bowl with a lime wedge to squeeze over the chili before eating.

 AT THE MARKET NOTE:

Chipotle peppers (which are smoked jalapeño peppers) are available dried or canned in a piquant tomato sauce (called *adobo*) and are sold at specialty food stores, Latin American markets, and in the Latin American foods section of many supermarkets. Use the canned ones in this recipe.

Fall Brodo with Acorn Squash, Swiss Chard, and Bacon

This soup's success depends on using a deeply-flavored broth (the *brodo* in the name), but don't worry if you don't have time to prepare the Made-from-Scratch Chicken Stock; the Shortcut Chicken Stock, which can be made in just half an hour, works beautifully, too. Sautéed onions, cubed acorn squash, and bow-shaped pasta called farfalle are cooked until tender in the rich broth; then chopped Swiss chard is added and simmered until wilted. Light yet satisfying, this Italian-inspired soup is garnished with a dusting of freshly grated Parmesan cheese and a sprinkle of crisp bacon.

SERVINGS: 6

PREP TIME:
30 to 40 minutes

START TO FINISH:
1½ hours

MAKE AHEAD:
Partially (The stock can be prepared ahead)

BREAD BASKET CHOICE:
Crusty peasant loaf, multigrain loaf, or ciabatta

SOUP-ER SIDE:
Arugula Salad Tossed with Parmesan Oil and Lemon (page 140), or omit bread and serve with Grilled Gorgonzola and Apple on Sourdough Bread (page 149) or Turkey Panini with White Cheddar and Cranberry Chutney (page 157)

1½- to 1¾-pound acorn squash

1 bunch (about 12 ounces) Swiss chard, preferably with dark green leaves and red stalks

6 slices good quality bacon, cut into ½-inch pieces

1⅓ cups chopped onion

8 cups Made-from-Scratch Chicken Stock (page 16) or Shortcut Chicken Stock (page 20)

1 cup farfalle (bow-tie pasta)

Kosher salt

1 to 2 pinches cayenne pepper

½ cup coarsely grated Parmesan cheese, preferably Parmigiano-Reggiano

1. Using a large, sharp knife, halve the squash lengthwise, and scoop out and discard the seeds and membranes. Then cut each half lengthwise into 4 segments. Using a vegetable peeler or small, sharp knife, peel the segments, and then cut them into ¾-inch cubes. Set aside.

2. Rinse the chard and pat dry. Cut off and discard the stalks. If the ribs on the leaves are more than a half-inch thick, cut them out and discard. Coarsely chop the chard to yield 4 loosely packed cups. Save any extra for another use.

3. In a large pot set over medium heat, sauté the bacon pieces until they are golden brown and crisp, for 3 to 4 minutes. Using a slotted spoon, remove bacon and drain on paper towels. Pour off all but 2 tablespoons of the bacon drippings in the pot and return the pot to medium heat. When hot, add the onions and sauté, stirring, until golden brown, for about 3 minutes.

continued on next page …

...continued

4. Add the stock and bring to a simmer. Add the squash and farfalle and cook until both the squash and pasta are tender, for 12 to 15 minutes, watching carefully to prevent overcooking. Add the chard and cook until it wilts, for 1 to 2 minutes more. Taste and season with salt, as needed, and cayenne pepper.

5. To serve, ladle soup into 6 shallow soup bowls. Pass bacon pieces and grated cheese separately in bowls. Serve immediately.

 AT THE MARKET NOTE:

Although I love to use acorn squash in this recipe, butternut squash can be substituted. Just make certain to cut it into ¾-inch (no larger) cubes. Or look for it already peeled and cubed in the produce section of many supermarkets.

Wild Mushroom Mélange

Three kinds of mushrooms—shiitake, porcini, and basic white ones—plus a handful of wild rice are simmered together slowly to form the base of this enticing soup. Shiitake and porcini mushrooms, savored for their meaty quality, add layers of earthy richness to the flavorful beef broth. Serve this mélange as a special first course or make it the centerpiece of a lunch or a light supper.

SERVINGS: 4

PREP TIME:
30 minutes

START TO FINISH:
1 hour 10 minutes

MAKE AHEAD
Partially

BREAD BASKET CHOICE:
Crusty baguette, country rosemary bread, or ciabatta

SOUP-ER SIDE:
Arugula Salad Tossed with Parmesan Oil and Lemon (page 140)

1½ ounces dried porcini mushrooms

2   tablespoons unsalted butter

2   tablespoons olive oil

8   ounces white mushrooms, sliced

3½ to 4 ounces shiitake mushrooms, stemmed and sliced

2   teaspoons kosher salt, plus more if needed

½   cup sliced shallots

1½ tablespoons minced garlic

1   teaspoon dried thyme

3   cups beef stock

¾   cup dry red wine

⅓   cup wild rice

Freshly ground black pepper

4   teaspoons chopped fresh flat-leaf parsley for garnish

 COOKING TIP:

It works best to prepare only the component parts of this soup in advance, combining them at the last minute. The mushrooms will act like sponges and absorb too much liquid if allowed to sit in the soup broth overnight.

---

1. Put the dried porcini mushrooms in a heatproof bowl and cover with 2 cups boiling water. Let stand until they are softened, for about 20 minutes. Strain the mushrooms in a strainer lined with a double thickness of paper towels, reserving the soaking liquid. Press down on the mushrooms and the paper towels to release any juices collected in them; it should yield about 1½ cups. If not, add enough water to equal this amount. Coarsely chop the porcini mushrooms.

2. Heat 2 tablespoons of the butter and the olive oil in a large, heavy pot set over medium heat. Add the sliced white mushrooms, shiitakes, and 2 teaspoons salt, and cook, stirring, for 3 minutes. Add the shallots and continue to cook, stirring, until mushrooms and shallots are softened and browned, for about 5 more minutes. Add garlic, thyme, and chopped porcinis; stir and cook 1 minute more. (The soup can be prepared 1 day ahead up to this point. Cool, cover, and refrigerate mushroom mixture and porcini soaking liquid separately. Reheat mushrooms over medium heat before continuing.)

3. Add 3 cups stock, wine, reserved porcini soaking liquid, and wild rice to the pot. Simmer, covered, until wild rice is tender, but still slightly crunchy to bite, for 40 to 50 minutes.

4. Taste soup and season with salt, as needed, plus several grinds of pepper. To serve, ladle soup into 4 bowls and sprinkle each serving with chopped parsley. Serve immediately.

Sweet Potato Soup with Orange Crème Fraîche

This velvety soup elevates the humble sweet potato to luxurious new heights. Roasting the potatoes first brings out their sweetness; when the roasted tubers are combined with fresh ginger and orange juice in the soup, they taste both exotic and deliciously decadent. Puréed and served with dollops of orange-scented crème fraîche, this soup could either begin or anchor a meal.

SERVINGS: 6

PREP TIME:
20 minutes

START TO FINISH:
1 hour

MAKE AHEAD:
Yes

BREAD BASKET CHOICE:
Crusty baguette, peasant loaf, whole-grain loaf, or ciabatta

SOUP-ER SIDE:
Roasted Pear, Walnut, and Feta Salad with Baby Greens (page 144), or omit bread and serve with Grilled Gorgonzola and Apple on Sourdough Bread (page 149) or Turkey Panini with White Cheddar and Cranberry Chutney (page 157)

ORANGE CRÈME FRAÎCHE

¾ cup crème fraîche (page 23)

¾ teaspoon finely minced peeled fresh ginger

¾ teaspoon grated orange zest

SOUP

4 tablespoons unsalted butter, divided

4½ cups peeled, cubed (½-inch dice) red-skinned sweet potatoes (1½ to 2 pounds; see note, facing page)

1½ teaspoons light brown sugar

2 cups chopped leeks, white and light green parts only (about 3 medium leeks)

⅔ cup finely chopped celery

¾ teaspoon minced peeled fresh ginger

6 cups chicken stock, plus extra if needed

⅔ cup fresh orange juice, plus extra if needed

Kosher salt

Ground white pepper

1 tablespoon chopped fresh flat-leaf parsley for garnish

1. *To make the crème fraîche:* In a medium bowl, whisk together the crème fraîche, ginger, and orange zest. (Orange crème fraîche can be prepared 1 day ahead; cover and refrigerate. Bring to room temperature for 30 minutes before using.)

2. *To make the soup:* Arrange an oven rack at center position and preheat oven to 400 degrees F. In a large, heavy skillet set over medium heat, melt 2 tablespoons butter. Add the cubed sweet potatoes and toss to coat with butter. Sprinkle with brown sugar, then spread sweet potato cubes in a single layer on a large, rimmed baking pan. Roast for 15 minutes, then stir and roast until tender when pierced with a knife and browned around the edges, for about 15 minutes more. Remove and set aside.

3. In a large, heavy pot set over medium heat, melt remaining 2 tablespoons butter. When hot, add leeks, celery, and fresh ginger, and sauté for 4 minutes, stirring occasionally. Add roasted sweet potatoes and sauté for 2 minutes more. Add chicken stock, orange juice, salt, and a generous pinch of white pepper. Bring mixture almost to a boil, then reduce heat and simmer until vegetables are very tender, for about 20 minutes or longer.

4. Purée the soup in batches in a food processor, blender, or food mill, and return soup to the pot. (Or use an immersion blender to purée the soup in the pot.) The soup will be quite thick; if it seems too thick, you can thin it with a half cup of chicken stock, plus 1 to 2 tablespoons fresh orange juice. Taste soup and season with salt, as needed, and white pepper. (The soup can be prepared 2 days ahead; cool, cover and refrigerate. Reheat, stirring, over medium heat.)

5. To serve, ladle soup into 6 shallow soup bowls. Using a ½-teaspoon measure, drop 5 to 6 generous dollops of crème fraîche atop each serving in a ring along the outside edge of the soup. With a small knife, swirl crème fraîche into soup to create a marbleized border. Sprinkle each serving with a little parsley.

 AT THE MARKET NOTE:

Sweet potatoes, a member of the morning glory family, come in many varieties, but two varieties are commonly available in our markets. One has tan skin and pale yellow, almost golden flesh that is somewhat dry. The other, often erroneously called "yams," has copper-colored skin and bright orange, moist flesh beneath. The latter variety works best in this recipe.

"About 30 Minutes" Chickpea and Pasta Soup with Rosemary

I make this soup in half an hour by multitasking. First, I assemble a quick-and-easy vegetable stock and simmer it for 10 minutes. While the stock is cooking, I measure and prep the chickpeas, pasta, rosemary, and spinach—then I stir them into the stock and cook until the pasta is al dente.

SERVINGS: 4

PREP TIME:
10 minutes

START TO FINISH:
30 minutes

MAKE AHEAD:
No

BREAD BASKET CHOICE:
Grissini (Italian bread sticks) or ciabatta

SOUP-ER SIDE:
Arugula Salad Tossed with Parmesan Oil and Lemon (page 140)

---

1 cup chopped leeks, white and light green parts only (1 to 2 medium leeks)

1 medium carrot, peeled and sliced

3 teaspoons kosher salt, divided, plus more if needed

1 bay leaf, broken in half

1 fresh thyme sprig or ½ teaspoon dried thyme

One 14½-ounce can diced tomatoes and their juices

One 15-ounce can chickpeas, drained and rinsed

1 cup small, short dried pasta, such as tubetti, ditalini, or mini-penne

2 teaspoons chopped fresh rosemary

3 ounces (about 3 cups) baby spinach leaves

One 3- to 4-ounce piece of Parmesan cheese, preferably Parmigiano-Reggiano, at room temperature (so that it will be easy to shave)

COOKING TIP:

This soup is best made and served immediately; as it sits, the pasta will continue to absorb the liquids. If, however, you happen to have leftover soup that has become too thick, thin it with some additional water.

---

1. Put the leeks, carrot, 2 teaspoons salt, the bay leaf, thyme sprig or dried thyme, tomatoes, and 4 cups water in a medium, heavy pot set over high heat. Bring mixture to a boil, then reduce heat and simmer for 10 minutes. Strain stock into large bowl, pressing down on the vegetables to extract as much liquid as possible, and return stock to pot (discard vegetables in strainer). It should yield about 4 cups. If not, add enough water to equal this amount.

2. Purée ½ cup chickpeas with ¼ cup water in a food processor or blender. Add the puréed chickpeas and remaining whole chickpeas, the pasta, chopped rosemary, and the remaining 1 teaspoon salt to the strained stock. Bring mixture to a simmer and cook, stirring occasionally, until pasta is al dente, for 6 to 8 minutes or longer, according to package directions. (If the soup starts to cook down too much, add 1 to 1½ cups additional water and return to simmer.) Add the spinach and cook 1 minute more or until wilted. Taste soup and season with salt, if needed.

3. To serve, ladle soup into 4 shallow soup bowls. Using a vegetable peeler, shave a generous amount of thin strips from the piece of Parmesan over each serving.

Roasted Tomato Soup with Garlic Croutons

Plum tomatoes are roasted until slightly charred and caramelized to form the base of this soup. This brings out their sweetness, producing a rich and concentrated flavor. Each serving is topped with toasted garlic croutons and a sprinkle of fresh basil or parsley. Offer this soup as a first course, or use it to anchor a light meal.

SERVINGS: 4

PREP TIME:
30 minutes

START TO FINISH:
1½ hours

MAKE AHEAD:
Yes

BREAD BASKET
CHOICE:
You don't need to offer bread with this soup since it is garnished with croutons.

SOUP-ER SIDE:
Arugula Salad Tossed with Parmesan Oil and Lemon (page 140)

3   pounds plum tomatoes
     (about 18 medium tomatoes)

2 ¼ teaspoons freshly ground black pepper

1 ⅛ teaspoons kosher salt, plus more if needed

¾   teaspoon crushed dried rosemary
     (see note, facing page)

3   large garlic cloves, minced

½   cup olive oil, plus extra for oiling the
     baking sheet

3 ½ cups chicken stock, divided

Garlic Croutons (facing page)

2   tablespoons finely chopped fresh basil or
     flat-leaf parsley

1. Arrange an oven rack at center position and preheat oven to 375 degrees F. Oil a heavy, rimmed baking sheet very generously with olive oil.

2. Halve tomatoes lengthwise and remove membranes, seeds, and stems. As you are preparing the tomatoes, place them cut-side down on a large plate or platter to drain.

3. In a large bowl, mix together the pepper, 1 ⅛ teaspoons salt, and the rosemary. Add the garlic and ½ cup olive oil and whisk well to blend. Add the tomatoes to the bowl and toss well to coat. Marinate tomatoes for 15 minutes.

4. Arrange the tomatoes, cut sides up, on prepared baking sheet. Drizzle any remaining oil in the bowl over them.

5. Roast until tomatoes are softened and are browned on the bottoms and around the edges, for 50 to 60 minutes, watching carefully to prevent overcooking. Remove baking sheet from oven.

6. Place half of the tomatoes in a food processor fitted with a metal blade. Pour in 1 cup of the stock and pulse until puréed, for about 1 minute.

7. Coarsely chop the remaining half of the tomatoes. In a medium, deep-sided saucepan, combine the chopped tomatoes, puréed tomato mixture, and remaining 2 ½ cups chicken

stock and bring just to a simmer over medium heat. (Don't worry about little bits of charred tomato pieces floating to the top—they add great flavor.) Taste soup and season with salt, as needed. (Soup can be prepared 1 day ahead; cool, cover, and refrigerate. Reheat over medium heat.)

8. To serve, ladle soup into 4 bowls. Garnish each serving with some croutons and a sprinkle of basil or parsley.

 AT THE MARKET NOTE:

To save time, buy crushed dried rosemary, rather than whole rosemary leaves that you must crush yourself. Crushed dried rosemary can be found in the spice section of most supermarkets. McCormick's brand is widely available.

Garlic Croutons

1½ tablespoons olive oil

1½ tablespoons unsalted butter

2 cups bread cubes (½-inch dice), made from good-quality French baguette or country bread, crusts included

1½ teaspoons minced garlic

1. In a medium, heavy skillet set over medium-high heat, heat the oil and butter until hot. Add the bread cubes and cook, stirring, until light golden, for about 3 minutes. Add garlic, stir, and cook for another 2 minutes until the bread is golden and crisp. Take care not to let the garlic bits burn. Remove from heat and set aside. (Croutons can be prepared 4 hours ahead; cover loosely with foil and leave at room temperature.)

Fabulous Fall Roots Soup

A trio of fall root vegetables—carrots, leeks, and a rutabaga—forms the savory foundation of this soup. Puréed and enriched with crème fraîche, this potage, with its velvety, smooth texture and glorious orange hue, is always a hit—whether it's a first course or the main attraction.

SERVINGS: 8

PREP TIME:
15 to 20 minutes

START TO FINISH:
1 hour

MAKE AHEAD:
Yes

BREAD BASKET CHOICE:
Crusty baguette, sourdough loaf, whole wheat loaf, or ciabatta

SOUP-ER SIDE:
Roasted Pear, Walnut, and Feta Salad with Baby Greens (page 144), or omit bread and serve with Turkey Panini with White Cheddar and Cranberry Chutney (page 157) or Grilled Gorgonzola and Apple on Sourdough Bread (page 149)

4   tablespoons unsalted butter

2½ cups chopped leeks, white and light green parts only (3 to 4 medium leeks)

1½ pounds carrots, peeled and diced

1   medium rutabaga (1 to 1¼ pounds), peeled and diced

8   cups chicken stock

Kosher salt

1¼ cups crème fraîche (page 23)

3   tablespoons finely chopped fresh flat-leaf parsley

AT THE MARKET NOTE:

Rutabagas, also known as yellow turnips or Swedes, are considered a member of the cabbage family. Large and round (3 to 5 inches in diameter) with a thin yellow skin and yellow flesh beneath, they are available year-round, with their prime season falling between July and April. Look for rutabagas that have smooth skin and that are firm and heavy for their size.

1. Heat butter in a large, heavy pot (with a lid) over medium-high heat. When melted and hot, add leeks, carrots, and rutabaga. Sauté vegetables until softened, for 10 minutes or longer. Add stock and bring mixture to a simmer. Reduce heat, cover, and simmer until vegetables are very tender, for about 30 minutes.

2. Purée the soup in batches in a food processor, blender, or food mill, and return soup to the pot. (Or use an immersion blender to purée the soup in the pot.) Whisk in ¾ cup of the crème fraîche. Taste soup and season with salt, as needed. (The soup can be prepared 2 days ahead. Cool, cover, and refrigerate. Reheat over medium heat.)

3. To serve, ladle soup into shallow soup bowls. Garnish each serving with a generous dollop of the remaining ½ cup crème fraîche and a sprinkling of parsley.

White Cheddar Creams with Crispy Bacon

A pinch of cayenne adds just a bit of kick to this smooth and creamy soup. Can you think of a better comfort food fix for a chilly day? In fact, you might like to pour it into a thermos for a fall tailgate or picnic. The bacon and green onion toppings can be packed separately and sprinkled on top at serving time.

3 tablespoons unsalted butter

1½ cups finely chopped onion

1 tablespoon minced garlic

¼ cup all-purpose flour

4½ cups chicken stock

1½ cups half-and-half

¼ teaspoon cayenne pepper

¼ cup dry white wine

12 ounces grated sharp white Cheddar cheese

Kosher salt

6 bacon slices, cut into 1-inch pieces and cooked until crisp and drained on paper towels

6 green onions, including 2 inches of green tops, coarsely chopped

1. Heat butter in a large, heavy pot set over medium heat. When hot, add the onion and sauté until softened, for 4 to 5 minutes. Add garlic and sauté 1 minute more. Sprinkle flour over the mixture and cook, stirring, for 2 minutes. Add the stock and half-and-half and bring mixture to a simmer.

2. Add the cayenne pepper and wine. Add the cheese, a little at a time, stirring until smooth after each addition. Taste soup and season with salt, as needed. (Soup can be prepared 1 day ahead; cool, cover, and refrigerate. Reheat over medium heat.)

3. To serve, ladle soup into 6 bowls and garnish each serving with bacon pieces and green onions.

Pumpkin Soup with Toasted Walnuts and Rosemary

Made with small pie pumpkins, which appear in supermarkets every fall, this soup has a silky texture and a subtle pumpkin flavor accented by a hint of rosemary and a pinch of cayenne. It is also quite versatile: I have served it as a first course, offered it as an entrée, and on some occasions even ladled it into espresso cups and passed them around as a prelude to an autumn dinner menu. Dollops of crème fraîche and toasted walnuts add distinctive accents as garnishes. When pumpkins aren't available, butternut squash can be substituted.

SERVINGS: 6

PREP TIME:
40 minutes

START TO FINISH:
1½ hours

MAKE AHEAD:
Yes

BREAD BASKET
CHOICE:
Whole-grain bread or
sourdough loaf

SOUP-ER SIDE:
Best-Ever Greens Salad
in Classic Vinaigrette
(page 139), made with
arugula or baby spinach

One 5-pound pie pumpkin (see note, facing page)

2   tablespoons unsalted butter

1½ cups chopped leeks, white and light green
     parts only (about 2 medium leeks)

6   cups chicken stock

2   teaspoons crushed dried rosemary
     (see note, facing page)

2   teaspoons kosher salt, plus more if needed

⅛   teaspoon cayenne pepper

1⅓ cups crème fraîche, divided (page 23)

⅓   cup walnuts, toasted and coarsely chopped
     (see tip, facing page)

6   fresh rosemary sprigs (optional)

1. Arrange an oven rack at center position and preheat oven to 400 degrees F.

2. Rinse and dry the pumpkin. Halve the pumpkin through the stem, and scoop out and discard the seeds and strings. Cut each half into large wedges, and then cut the wedges into 3- to 4-inch pieces. Place the pumpkin pieces, cut sides down, in a large, heavy baking pan. Add enough water to the pan to measure ¼ inch up the sides. Cover tightly with aluminum foil.

3. Bake until pumpkin is tender when pierced with a sharp knife, for 45 to 50 minutes. Remove from oven and let cool.

4. When pumpkin is cool enough to handle comfortably, use a small, sharp knife to remove skin. Cut the pieces into 1-inch cubes to yield 8 cups. (Save any remaining pumpkin for another use.)

5. Heat butter in a large, heavy pan (with a lid) over medium heat. When hot, add leeks and cook, stirring, until they are softened and translucent, for about 3 minutes. Add the pumpkin cubes,

stock, rosemary, 2 teaspoons salt, and cayenne pepper. Stir to combine and bring mixture to a simmer. Reduce heat, cover, and cook for 10 minutes to meld flavors.

6. Purée the soup in batches in a food processor, blender, or food mill, and return soup to the pot. (Or use an immersion blender to purée the soup in the pot.) Whisk in 1 cup of the crème fraîche. Taste soup and season with salt, as needed. (Soup can be prepared 2 days ahead. Cool, cover, and refrigerate. Reheat over low heat.)

7. To serve, ladle soup into 6 soup bowls. Garnish each serving with a dollop of the remaining ⅓ cup crème fraîche and sprinkle with chopped walnuts. If desired, garnish each serving with a rosemary sprig.

 AT THE MARKET NOTES:

Pie pumpkins are a variety of pumpkins that are harvested as they become soccer ball size. They are sweet and have more succulent flesh than larger pumpkins, which are best used for decorative purposes. Pie pumpkins, as their name implies, are great used in pumpkin pies and in pumpkin soups like this one.

When pumpkins are not available, you can substitute 8 cups diced peeled butternut squash. Skip the oven-cooking step and simply add the diced squash to the pot when you add the leeks, sauté them together for about 6 minutes, and then proceed with the recipe, cooking the soup until the squash cubes are tender, for about 25 minutes.

To save time, buy crushed dried rosemary, rather than whole rosemary leaves that you must crush yourself. Crushed rosemary can be found in the spice section of most supermarkets. McCormick's brand is widely available.

 COOKING TIP:

To toast walnuts, spread them on a rimmed baking sheet and place in a preheated 350 degrees F oven until lightly browned and fragrant, for 5 to 6 minutes, watching carefully to prevent burning.

Tortilla Soup with Chicken, Lime, and Smoked Chilies

Tortilla soups can vary from thick, tomatoey purées to lighter versions like this one. Bits of tender chicken float in a clear broth flavored with tomatoes, Mexican herbs and spices, and a smoky chipotle pepper. Crisp tortilla strips and dollops of sour cream are delicious finishing touches.

SERVINGS: 6

PREP TIME:
30 minutes

START TO FINISH:
1 hour 15 minutes

MAKE AHEAD:
Yes

BREAD BASKET CHOICE:
You don't need to offer bread with this soup since it is garnished with tortilla strips.

SOUP-ER SIDE:
Red, Yellow, and Orange Pepper Salad with Tequila-Lime Dressing (page 148)

1	small dried chipotle pepper (see note, page 48)
1½	tablespoons olive oil, plus extra for frying the tortilla strips
1	cup chopped onion
1	tablespoon minced garlic
2	teaspoons ground cumin
1½	teaspoons dried oregano
	One 28-ounce can diced tomatoes, drained well
6	cups chicken stock
1	pound boneless, skinless chicken breast, cut into 1-inch pieces
1	medium yellow bell pepper, stemmed, seeded, and cut into julienned strips about 1 inch long by ¼ inch wide
2	tablespoons fresh lime juice
	Kosher salt
	Six 6- to 7-inch corn tortillas
	½ to ¾ cup sour cream
⅓	cup chopped fresh cilantro
6	thin lime wedges for garnish (optional)

1. Put the chipotle pepper in a small bowl and cover with 1 cup boiling water. Let it sit until softened, for about 20 minutes. Drain pepper, discarding water, and pat dry. Using a small, sharp knife, cut a lengthwise slit in pepper and scrape out and discard seeds (see page 22). Coarsely chop pepper and set aside.

2. Heat 1½ tablespoons olive oil in a large, heavy pot over medium heat. When hot, add onion and cook until softened, stirring often, for 4 to 5 minutes. Add garlic and cook, stirring, for 1 minute more. Add chopped chipotle, cumin, oregano, tomatoes, and stock. Bring mixture to a simmer and cook for 10 minutes. Purée the soup in a food processor, blender, or food mill, and return soup to the pot. (Or use an immersion blender to purée the soup in the pot.)

3. Bring puréed soup to a simmer over medium heat and add the chicken and yellow peppers. Simmer until chicken is cooked through and peppers are tender, for about 5 minutes. Stir in the lime juice, then taste and season with salt, as needed. (Soup can be prepared 1 day ahead; cool, cover, and refrigerate. Reheat over medium heat.)

continued on next page . . .

…continued

4. To make the garnish, stack the tortillas, then cut them in half. Stack halves and cut crosswise into ¼-inch-wide strips. Set a medium skillet over medium-high heat and coat the bottom generously with olive oil. When oil is hot, add one-third of the tortilla strips and sauté, turning often, until golden and crisp, for 3 to 4 minutes. Using slotted spoon, transfer strips to paper towels to drain. Repeat with remaining tortilla strips in 2 more batches, adding more oil as needed. (Tortilla strips can be cooked 3 hours ahead; leave at room temperature.)

5. To serve, ladle soup into 6 soup bowls. Garnish each serving with a generous handful of fried tortilla strips. Add a dollop of sour cream and a sprinkle of cilantro, and serve with a lime wedge to squeeze over the soup, if desired.

 AT THE MARKET NOTE:

For this soup, I like to use dried chipotles (dried smoked jalapeño peppers), which are sold in cellophane packages at most supermarkets, usually in the produce section. (See note about handling hot peppers on page 22.) If you can't find dried chipotles, substitute canned chipotles in *adobo*, a spicy tomato sauce. Rinse off the sauce and seed and chop the pepper before adding it to the soup. Chipotle peppers in *adobo* sauce are sold at specialty food stores, Latin American markets, and in the Latin American foods section of many supermarkets.

Scallop and Corn Chowder

I like to make this soup in early fall, when the temperatures are just starting to drop and the days are suddenly cooler. I pair the last of the year's fresh corn with sea scallops that are dusted with smoked paprika, cumin, and pepper. Other chowder mainstays—potatoes, bacon, and onion—also contribute to the delectable taste and enticing texture of this soup.

SERVINGS: 6

PREP TIME:
20 minutes

START TO FINISH:
50 minutes

MAKE AHEAD:
Partially

BREAD BASKET CHOICE:
Crusty hard rolls

SOUP-ER SIDE:
Best-Ever Greens Salad in Classic Vinaigrette (page 139), made with mixed greens

1   pound large red-skin potatoes, peeled and cut into ½-inch dice

4   cups fresh corn kernels or frozen thawed corn kernels, divided

2   cups chicken stock, divided

8   thick smoked bacon slices, cut into ¼-inch pieces

1   cup chopped onion

1⅓   cups half-and-half

Kosher salt

1   pound large sea scallops, side muscles removed

1½   teaspoons Spanish smoked paprika (see note, page 50)

1½   teaspoons ground cumin

¾   teaspoon freshly ground black pepper

⅛   teaspoon cayenne pepper

Vegetable or olive oil for cooking the scallops

2   tablespoons chopped fresh chives

1. Bring a medium pot of water to a boil over high heat. Add potatoes and cook until just tender when pierced with a knife, for about 10 minutes. Drain potatoes and set aside.

2. Purée 2 cups of the corn kernels with 1 cup of the chicken stock in a food processor or blender and set aside.

3. In a large, heavy pot set over medium heat, sauté the bacon until crisp. Using a slotted spoon, transfer bacon to paper towels to drain. Pour off all but 1 tablespoon drippings in pot. Add onion and remaining 2 cups of corn kernels. Sauté, stirring, until onions are softened and corn starts to brown lightly, for 5 to 6 minutes.

4. Stir in the remaining 1 cup chicken stock and the puréed corn mixture. Reduce heat to a simmer and cook for 10 minutes. Add potatoes, bacon, and half-and-half and cook for 2 to 3 minutes more. Do not let the soup come to a boil. (Soup can be prepared 1 day ahead to this point; cool, cover, and refrigerate. Reheat over low heat and proceed with recipe.) Remove pot from the heat; taste soup and season with salt, as needed. Cover to keep warm while you prepare the scallops.

continued on next page…

...continued

5. Pat scallops dry, then quarter them. In a small bowl, mix together smoked paprika, cumin, black pepper, and cayenne; spread spice mixture on a dinner plate. Coat the scallops on all sides with the spice mixture.

6. Add enough olive oil to coat the bottom of a large, heavy skillet set over medium-high heat. When hot, add enough scallops to fit comfortably in the pan (do not crowd) and sauté for 1 to 2 minutes per side, until just seared. Transfer scallops to plate. Repeat with remaining scallops. Season scallops with salt.

7. To serve, ladle the chowder into 6 soup bowls and top with scallops, dividing evenly. Garnish each serving with some chopped chives.

 AT THE MARKET NOTE:

Spanish smoked paprika, called *pimentón*, is available at gourmet food stores and some well-stocked supermarkets. Look for *dulce* (sweet) on the label, which indicates a mildly spiced paprika. If you can't find smoked paprika locally, you can order it from La Tienda (www.tienda.com).

Apple Soup with Crumbled Roquefort and Bacon

Elegant, rich, and creamy, this soup makes a tempting opener for a fall menu, followed by roast pork or chicken. It also makes a fine centerpiece for a light lunch or supper. This soup will also be a favorite among those who love to cook in advance because it tastes even better when prepared a day ahead.

SERVINGS: 6

PREP TIME:
25 to 30 minutes

START TO FINISH:
1 hour

MAKE AHEAD:
Yes

BREAD BASKET
CHOICE:
Crusty baguette or
peasant loaf

SOUP-ER SIDE:
Best-Ever Greens Salad
in Classic Vinaigrette
(page 139), made
with baby spinach or
mixed greens

3   large Red Delicious apples (about 1½ pounds)
3   large Granny Smith apples (about 1½ pounds)
4   tablespoons unsalted butter
1   cup chopped onion
1   teaspoon finely chopped garlic
5   cups chicken stock
1   cup heavy or whipping cream
¼   cup apple brandy, such as Calvados or
     applejack (see note)

Kosher salt

GARNISH
3   ounces Roquefort cheese or other blue
    cheese, such as Stilton or Bleu d'Auvergne,
    crumbled
3   tablespoons unsalted butter, cut into
    small pieces
3   bacon slices, cooked until crisp, drained
    on paper towels, and crumbled
6   thin Red Delicious apple slices, tossed in
    1 teaspoon fresh lemon juice
6   thin Granny Smith apple slices, tossed in
    1 teaspoon fresh lemon juice
2   tablespoons chopped fresh chives

1. Peel, core, and thinly slice the Red Delicious and Granny Smith apples. Heat 4 tablespoons butter in a large, heavy pot set over medium heat. When hot, add the apple slices, onion, and garlic and sauté, stirring, for 5 minutes. Add the stock and bring mixture to a simmer. Cook at a simmer, uncovered, until apples and onions are tender, for 20 to 25 minutes.

2. Purée the soup in batches in a food processor, blender, or food mill, and return soup to the pot. (Or use an immersion blender to purée the soup in the pot.) Whisk in the cream and apple brandy. Bring to a simmer, and season with salt, as needed. Do not let the soup come to a boil. (The soup can be made 1 day ahead; cool, cover, and refrigerate. Reheat over medium heat.)

3. *For the garnish:* In a small bowl, toss together the crumbled Roquefort, small pieces of butter, and crumbled bacon; set aside.

4. To serve, ladle soup into 6 bowls and garnish each serving with one slice each of Red Delicious and Granny Smith apples. Spoon some of the crumbled Roquefort-bacon mixture in the center of each serving. Sprinkle with chopped chives.

 AT THE MARKET NOTE:
Apple brandy adds a subtle, but important, flavor to this soup. Calvados is available in better liquor stores. Applejack is more widely available where spirits are sold.

French Lentil Soup with Garlic Sausage

Served chunky and unadorned, this simple, peasant-style soup is perfect to offer on a chilly fall evening. The best lentils for this potage are Puy lentils from France. They have a robust flavor and retain their shape well when cooked. In the following recipe, these green lentils are paired with bits of kielbasa, a hearty garlic-scented sausage, and seasoned with a mirepoix—the sauté of diced onion, carrot, and celery that underpins so many soups and stews.

SERVINGS: 6

PREP TIME:
15 minutes

START TO FINISH:
1 hour 15 minutes

MAKE AHEAD:
Yes

BREAD BASKET CHOICE:
Crusty baguette, sourdough, or whole wheat loaf

SOUP-ER SIDE:
Best-Ever Greens Salad in Classic Vinaigrette (page 139), made with red leaf lettuce

2	tablespoons olive oil
1	cup diced carrots (¼-inch dice)
½	cup chopped onion
½	cup diced celery (¼-inch dice)
3	medium garlic cloves, smashed and peeled
6	ounces garlic sausage, such as kielbasa, cut into ¼-inch dice
2	teaspoons dried thyme
9	cups beef stock
2	bay leaves, broken in half
1	pound (2 cups) Puy lentils (French green lentils; see note)

Kosher salt

¼ cup chopped fresh flat-leaf parsley for garnish

 AT THE MARKET NOTE:

French Green lentils, known as Puy lentils, can be found in some supermarkets (such as Whole Foods and Wild Oats) and in specialty food stores.

1. Heat oil in a large pot (with a lid) over medium heat. When hot, add the carrots, onion, and celery. Cook, stirring often, until the vegetables are just softened, for about 5 minutes. Add the garlic, sausage, and thyme, and cook 1 minute more.

2. Add the stock and bay leaves, and bring mixture to a simmer over high heat. Stir in the lentils, then reduce heat, cover, and cook at a gentle simmer until tender, for about 50 minutes.

3. Remove and discard the bay leaves. Remove the garlic pieces and transfer to food processor. Using a slotted spoon, strain ½ cup solids (vegetables and sausage) from the soup and purée them with garlic pieces in a food processor, or combine them with garlic pieces in a small bowl and smash with the back of a fork. Stir the puréed mixture into the pot; this will thicken the soup slightly. Taste soup and season with salt, as needed. (Soup can be prepared 1 day ahead; cool, cover, and refrigerate. Reheat over medium heat.)

4. To serve, ladle the soup into 6 soup bowls and sprinkle some parsley over each serving.

3 Winter

DECEMBER | JANUARY | FEBRUARY

Winter opens on a spirited note, as December ushers in the holiday season. Then, just as the sparkle of celebrations dims, winter lays its claim. Short days and cold winds conspire to drive us indoors for the long haul. During these months, I find solace in the produce aisle at the supermarket. Far from barren, the shelves offer a cornucopia of humble riches this time of year. Root vegetables abound: Carrots, parsnips, leeks, celery, and potatoes are always available, as are hearty greens likes cabbage and kale. Paired with such staples as beans and pasta or combined with bits of smoky bacon and sausage, these ingredients become the inspiration for many of my winter soups.

In this chapter, you'll find recipes based on the winter larder, which are perfect for Christmas holiday celebrations and for the cold months that follow. Creamy Celery Bisque with Stilton Toasts is both festive and easy to make—a winning combination for Christmas and New Year celebrations. Or try pozole, a vibrant Mexican Christmas soup made with hominy and fork-tender chicken. Served with an array of colorful garnishes, it bursts with bright, clear flavors.

If you're planning a party for the Super Bowl, the Oscars, or Mardi Gras, you'll find soups in this chapter for each of these special winter occasions. Spicy Pork Chili with Cumin Polenta will get cheers from football fans, and Gulf Coast Shrimp Gumbo is packed with authentic flavor for a Fat Tuesday fête.

As befits the season, many of the recipes that follow might be described as "big"—hearty meals in a bowl that are good for warming the soul as well as the body. Ribollita, "Melt in Your Mouth" Beef and Barley Soup, and White Bean Soup with Chorizo and Kale all fall in this category.

Any of the satisfying soups in this chapter would make a perfect winter meal. Simply add a salad and warm bread to complete the menu. Then light a fire, pull up a chair, and dip your spoon into a steaming bowl of soup. With each taste, you'll be reminded how delicious winter can be.

White Bean Soup with Chorizo and Kale

Rich and filling, this soup was created by my friend Madeleine Blais, a Pulitzer Prize–winning journalist and inveterate hostess. It was the star attraction at a soup party she and I hosted with our spouses one cold, wintry New England night. We watched with delight as guests asked for seconds—then thirds—of this unpretentious potage. The base is made with white beans that are slowly simmered in stock with salt pork and vegetables. Garlic and red pepper flakes add robust accents, as do smoky chorizo slices. At serving time, handfuls of chopped kale are stirred into the soup and quickly cooked. This soup is definitely a meal in itself.

SERVINGS: 6

PREP TIME:
50 minutes, plus 1 hour for soaking the beans

START TO FINISH:
2 hours 40 minutes, plus 1 hour for soaking the beans

MAKE AHEAD:
Yes

BREAD BASKET CHOICE:
A crusty multigrain loaf, a sourdough loaf, or rosemary focaccia

SOUP-ER SIDE:
Arugula Salad Tossed with Parmesan Oil and Lemon (page 140)

1	pound dried great Northern beans
One 4-ounce piece salt pork	
3	tablespoons olive oil
2	cups chopped onion
2	cups shredded carrots (see note, facing page)
2	cups chopped celery
5	large garlic cloves, peeled and chopped
1	tablespoon dried thyme
Scant ½ teaspoon red pepper flakes, plus more if needed	
½	teaspoon kosher salt, plus more if needed
Freshly ground black pepper	
10 to 12 cups chicken stock	
8	ounces Spanish chorizo, thinly sliced (see note, facing page)
5	cups (loosely packed) chopped fresh kale, stems cut off and discarded
¾	cup grated Parmesan cheese, preferably Parmigiano-Reggiano

1. Rinse and sort through the beans to remove any pebbles. Put beans in a large heatproof bowl; cover with 8 cups of boiling water. Soak beans for 1 hour. Rinse the salt pork under cold running water and cut it into 4 equal pieces.

2. While the beans are soaking, heat the olive oil in a large, deep-sided pot (with a lid) over medium heat. When hot, add onion, carrots, and celery. Cook, stirring, until vegetables are softened, for 6 to 8 minutes. Add garlic and cook, stirring, for 2 minutes more. Remove from heat and set aside.

3. After beans have soaked, drain and rinse them in a colander. Transfer beans to the pot with the sautéed vegetables and add the salt pork. Stir in the thyme, red pepper flakes, ½ teaspoon salt, several grinds of pepper, and 10 cups of the stock.

4. Set the pot over medium-high heat and bring mixture to a simmer. Reduce heat, cover pot, and cook for 1 hour. Add chorizo, and cook, covered, for 30 minutes more or until beans

are just tender. Using a slotted spoon, remove and discard the salt pork. (The soup can be prepared to this point 2 days ahead. Cool, cover, and refrigerate. Reheat over medium heat.)

5. Taste soup and season with salt and black pepper, as needed, and add an extra pinch of red pepper flakes, if desired. If soup is too thin, cook it over high heat for a few minutes to reduce broth and thicken slightly. If it is too thick, dilute it with the remaining stock and heat the soup for a few more minutes.

6. Add the kale to the simmering soup, and cook until it is wilted, for about 3 minutes.

7. To serve, ladle soup into 6 large soup bowls and garnish each serving with a generous sprinkling of Parmesan cheese. Pass any extra cheese in a bowl.

 AT THE MARKET NOTES:

To save a little time, I pick up some shredded carrots from the salad bar at my local market. Many supermarkets also carry bags of shredded carrots in the produce section.

Chorizo is a highly seasoned pork sausage available in both Spanish and Mexican varieties. For this recipe, use the firmer smoked Spanish type, which is made with pork that is already cooked. (Mexican chorizo is prepared with fresh pork enclosed in a casing.) Chorizo is available at Spanish markets, specialty food stores, and some supermarkets, such as Whole Foods.

 COOKING TIP:

When this soup is made ahead and refrigerated or frozen, the beans sometimes absorb more of the liquid, which will thicken the soup. Thin it with extra stock, if necessary.

Cold Weather Potato Chowder with Caraway Cheese

This chowder, which is prepared traditionally with bacon, onions, and potatoes that are simmered in a mixture of stock and milk, is enriched with a final addition of grated Havarti cheese studded with caraway seeds. The buttery cheese blends beautifully with all the ingredients, plus it adds an extra hint of creaminess to the soup's texture.

SERVINGS: 4

PREP TIME:
10 minutes

START TO FINISH:
30 to 35 minutes

MAKE AHEAD:
Partially

BREAD BASKET
CHOICE:
Pumpernickel or
unseeded rye

SOUP-ER SIDE:
Omit bread and
serve with Roast Beef
and Watercress with
Horseradish Cream on
Dark Bread (page 151)

4   slices (4 ounces) bacon, cut into
    ½-inch pieces

½   cup chopped onion

½   cup diced celery

1   pound red-skin potatoes, scrubbed but not
    peeled, cut into ½-inch dice

1   tablespoon minced garlic

2   cups chicken stock

2   cups whole milk

1   cup (4 ounces) Havarti cheese with caraway
    seeds, coarsely grated

1   tablespoon unsalted butter at room
    temperature

1   tablespoon all-purpose flour

Kosher salt

Freshly ground black pepper

2   tablespoons chopped fresh chives for garnish

1. Sauté bacon in a large, heavy pot set over medium heat until browned and crisp, for 3 to 4 minutes. Using slotted spoon, transfer bacon to paper towels to drain. Pour out and discard all but 2 tablespoons bacon drippings.

2. Add onion and celery to the bacon drippings in the pot and cook, stirring frequently, until softened, for 4 to 5 minutes. Add diced potatoes and sauté for 2 minutes. Add garlic and sauté, stirring, for 1 minute.

3. Add chicken stock and milk to pot and bring mixture to a simmer. Cook soup at a simmer until the potatoes are tender, for 10 to 15 minutes. Do not let soup come to a boil. (Soup can be prepared to this point 1 day ahead. Cool, cover, and refrigerate. Reheat over low heat and proceed with recipe.)

4. When ready to serve, add the cheese, a little at a time, to the hot soup, stirring until melted after each addition. In a small bowl, mix the butter and flour with a fork to make a paste. Whisk this mixture into the soup, a little at a time, and cook until completely blended, for 1 to 2 minutes. Taste soup and season with salt and freshly ground pepper, as needed.

5. To serve, ladle soup into 4 bowls and sprinkle each serving with chopped bacon and chives.

Tomato and Fennel Soup with Pernod Cream

Tomato and fennel team up fabulously in this soup. The sweetness of the tomato is complemented by the licorice accent of the fennel. Dollops of crème fraîche scented with Pernod—the celebrated anise-scented liqueur so beloved in the south of France—add another hit of licorice flavor while beautifully garnishing the soup. (But don't worry if you don't have Pernod on hand. The soup will still be delicious adorned simply with crème fraîche.)

SERVINGS: 6

PREP TIME:
20 minutes

START TO FINISH:
45 to 50 minutes

MAKE AHEAD:
Yes

BREAD BASKET CHOICE:
Crusty baguette or sourdough loaf

SOUP-ER SIDE:
Arugula Salad Tossed with Parmesan Oil and Lemon (page 140), or omit bread and serve with Crab and Avocado Sandwiches (page 155) or Vegetable Pitas with Goat Cheese and Fresh Herbs (page 152)

4	medium fennel bulbs
¼	cup olive oil
1	cup chopped onion
½	cup diced carrot
2	tablespoons chopped fresh tarragon, plus 6 sprigs for garnish
1	teaspoon kosher salt, plus more if needed
¼	teaspoon red pepper flakes
1	28-ounce can diced tomatoes, drained well
4	cups chicken stock
⅔	cup crème fraîche (page 23), divided
¾	teaspoon Pernod (optional)

1. Cut off and discard stalks (if attached) from fennel. Halve the bulbs lengthwise, and cut out and discard the tough inner cores. Chop enough fennel to yield 3 cups.

2. Heat the oil in a large, deep-sided pot over medium-high heat. When hot, add the chopped fennel, onion, and carrot, and cook, stirring frequently, until vegetables are softened and starting to brown, for 8 to 10 minutes. Stir in the chopped tarragon, 1 teaspoon salt, and the red pepper flakes. Add the tomatoes and chicken stock, and continue to cook at a gentle simmer (reducing heat slightly, if necessary) until the vegetables are tender, for about 20 minutes.

3. Purée the soup in batches in a food processor, blender, or food mill, and return soup to the pot. (Or use an immersion blender to purée the soup in the pot.) Ladle a little of the warm soup into a small bowl and whisk in ⅓ cup of the crème fraîche. Then whisk this mixture into the soup. Taste soup and season with salt, as needed. (The soup can be prepared 1 day ahead. Cool, cover, and refrigerate. Reheat over medium heat.)

4. To serve, ladle one cup of soup into each of 6 bowls. If desired, whisk Pernod with the remaining ⅓ cup crème fraîche in a small bowl. Garnish the center of each serving with a dollop of crème fraîche (with or without the Pernod) and a fresh tarragon sprig.

Cauliflower Soup with Crispy Prosciutto and Parmesan

Who would believe that cauliflower—the vegetable Mark Twain called "cabbage with a college education"—could be used to create such a luxuriously smooth soup with a sophisticated taste? The snowy white florets are paired with leeks, and cooked in stock until tender; then the mixture is puréed and enriched with crème fraîche and Parmesan cheese. Thin strips of crisp prosciutto sprinkled on top add great color and texture—as well as a delicious salty punch.

SERVINGS: 6

PREP TIME:
20 minutes

START TO FINISH:
40 minutes

MAKE AHEAD:
Yes

BREAD BASKET CHOICE:
Crusty baguette or ciabatta

SOUP-ER SIDE:
Best-Ever Greens Salad in Classic Vinaigrette (page 139) or Arugula Salad Tossed with Parmesan Oil and Lemon (page 140)

4	tablespoons unsalted butter
3	cups chopped leeks, white and light green parts only (4 to 5 medium leeks)
12	cups cauliflower florets (from 2 large heads; about 2 pounds each)
8	cups chicken stock
1/8	teaspoon cayenne pepper
1	cup grated Parmesan cheese, divided
1/2	cup crème fraîche (page 23)
	Kosher salt
4	ounces thinly sliced prosciutto
1	tablespoon olive oil
1/2	cup chopped fresh flat-leaf parsley

1. Melt the butter in a large, heavy deep-sided pot (with a lid) set over medium-high heat. Add the leeks and sauté, stirring, until softened, for 4 to 5 minutes. Add the cauliflower florets, chicken stock, and cayenne pepper. Bring to a simmer, stirring occasionally, then reduce heat to a gentle simmer and cover pot. Cook until vegetables are very tender, for about 20 minutes.

2. Purée the soup in batches in a food processor, blender, or food mill, and return soup to the pot. (Or use an immersion blender to purée the soup in the pot.) Whisk in 1/2 cup of the cheese and the crème fraîche. Taste soup and season with salt, as needed. (The soup can be made 2 days ahead; cool, cover, and refrigerate. Reheat over medium heat.)

3. Cut the prosciutto into julienne strips 3 to 4 inches long and 1/4 inch wide. Heat the olive oil in a medium skillet set over medium heat. When hot, add the prosciutto and sauté, stirring constantly, until crisp and browned, for 4 to 5 minutes. Using slotted spoon, transfer prosciutto to paper towels to drain.

4. To serve, ladle soup into 6 soup bowls and sprinkle each serving with some prosciutto, chopped parsley, and remaining 1/2 cup Parmesan.

Cream of Chicken and Fennel Soup

Rich and satisfying, this chicken soup gets an unexpected yet delicious infusion of flavor from fennel. Both chopped fennel bulbs and crushed fennel seeds provide a nice anise-scented touch to this extra smooth and creamy potage.

SERVINGS: 4

PREP TIME:
15 minutes

START TO FINISH:
1 hour

MAKE AHEAD:
Partially

BREAD BASKET CHOICE:
Biscuits or crusty hard rolls

SOUP-ER SIDE:
Roasted Pear, Walnut, and Feta Salad with Baby Greens (page 144)

2   medium fennel bulbs

4   cups chicken stock, plus ½ to 1 cup extra

1½ cups (about 8 ounces) sliced baby carrots

2   cups diced cooked chicken, preferably more white than dark meat (see note, page 64)

2½ tablespoons unsalted butter

2½ tablespoons all-purpose flour

1½ cups light cream

2   tablespoons fresh lemon juice

2   teaspoons fennel seeds, crushed (see tip, page 64)

1 teaspoon kosher salt, plus more if needed

1   cup (2½ to 3 ounces) snow peas

3   tablespoons chopped fresh flat-leaf parsley (optional)

1. Cut off stalks from fennel (if attached) and reserve feathery tops for garnish, if desired. (Reserve tops in a glass of water to prevent wilting.) Halve bulbs lengthwise; cut out and discard tough cores. Chop enough fennel to yield 1½ cups.

2. Bring 4 cups chicken stock to a simmer in a large pot set over medium-high heat. Add fennel and carrots, and cook until vegetables are tender when pierced with a knife, for about 12 minutes.

3. Drain the fennel and carrots, reserving 1½ cups of the stock. (Save any extra stock for another use.) Put the fennel, carrots, and diced chicken in a large bowl.

4. Melt butter in a large, heavy saucepan set over medium-high heat. Add flour and cook, stirring, for 1 minute or less. Gradually whisk in cream and reserved 1½ cups stock. Whisk until mixture thickens slightly and coats the back of a spoon, for 4 minutes or longer. Stir in lemon juice, fennel seeds, and 1 teaspoon salt. Stir in chicken, fennel, and carrots. If the soup is too thick, thin it with additional stock as needed. (The soup can be prepared 1 day ahead; cool, cover, and refrigerate. Reheat over medium heat.)

continued on next page…

...continued

5. When ready to serve the soup, trim and discard ends from snow peas. Cut the snow peas on the diagonal into thirds. Add the snow peas to the soup, and cook just until just tender, for about 2 minutes. Taste soup and season with salt, as needed.

6. To serve, ladle soup into 4 soup bowls. Garnish each serving with a sprig from the fennel tops or with some chopped parsley.

 AT THE MARKET NOTE:

Save yourself a little prep time by picking up a plain or herb-seasoned roast chicken from the deli section of the supermarket.

 COOKING TIP:

You can crush fennel seeds in an electric spice grinder, or place in a mortar and crush finely with a pestle, or seal them in a plastic bag and pound with a meat mallet or rolling pin. The seeds should be finely crushed.

Ribollita—The Tuscan Minestrone

Ribollita means "boiled again" in Italian, and this hearty peasant vegetable soup does, in fact, get a double dose of cooking. Traditionally, the Tuscan-style minestrone is made on one day, then the leftover soup is reheated the next day and thickened with chunks of day-old crusty Italian bread or served over thick slices of toasted bread, which soften in the broth and absorb the delicious vegetable flavors. There are countless versions, of course, but most include day-old bread, cannellini beans, and *cavolo nero* (black kale, which can be replaced with Savoy cabbage). I like to top each portion with a drizzle of olive oil and a sprinkling of freshly grated Parmesan cheese. True to its name, this soup tastes even better when it's prepared a day or two ahead and reheated before serving.

SERVINGS: 6

PREP TIME:
1 hour

START TO FINISH:
2 ½ to 3 hours

MAKE AHEAD:
Yes

BREAD BASKET CHOICE:
You don't need to offer bread with this soup because each serving includes a slice of toasted garlic bread.

SOUP-ER SIDE:
Arugula Salad Tossed with Parmesan Oil and Lemon (page 140)

8   ounces (1 cup) dried great Northern or cannellini beans

3   tablespoons olive oil, plus extra for garnish

1   cup chopped onion

½   cup chopped leek, white and light green parts only (about 1 medium leek)

½   cup diced carrot (½-inch dice)

½   cup diced celery (½-inch dice)

1   tablespoon minced garlic

1   teaspoon crushed dried rosemary (see note, page 66)

One 14 ½-ounce can diced tomatoes and their juices

8 to 10 ounces Savoy cabbage (from 1 head), halved, cored, and cut into ¼-inch-wide strips to make 2 ½ to 3 cups

1 ½ tablespoons kosher salt, plus more if needed

8   ounces russet or Yukon gold potato (1 medium), peeled and cut into ½-inch dice

8   ounces zucchini (1 medium), halved length-wise and cut into ½-inch-thick slices

6   ounces Swiss chard, stems removed and leaves cut into ½-inch-thick strips to make 2 cups

8   ½-inch-thick slices day-old Italian bread, such as ciabatta

1 to 2 whole garlic cloves, peeled and halved

1   cup grated Parmesan cheese, preferably Parmigiano-Reggiano, for garnish

1. Rinse and sort through the beans to remove any pebbles. Put beans in a large bowl; cover with 3 cups of boiling water. Soak beans for 1 hour. Drain beans in a colander and reserve.

2. Heat olive oil in a large, heavy pot (with a lid) over medium-high heat. When hot, add the onion, leek, carrot, and celery and sauté until just softened, for 3 to 4 minutes. Add minced garlic and rosemary and sauté 1 minute more.

continued on next page…

...continued

3. Add 8 cups water, the reserved beans, tomatoes, cabbage, and 1½ tablespoons salt. Bring to a boil, then reduce heat and cook at a simmer, covered, for 1 hour.

4. Add potatoes, zucchini, and chard; simmer, covered, until the potatoes and zucchini are tender and the chard has wilted, for 20 to 25 minutes. Taste soup and season with salt, as needed. (Soup can be prepared 2 days ahead. Cool, cover, and refrigerate. Reheat over medium heat.)

5. When ready to serve, lightly toast the bread slices, then rub each piece on both sides with a cut garlic clove. Either place 1 bread slice in the bottom of 6 soup bowls and ladle soup over or ladle soup into 6 bowls and top each with a bread slice. Garnish each serving with Parmesan cheese and a drizzle of olive oil.

 AT THE MARKET NOTE:

To save time, buy crushed dried rosemary, rather than whole rosemary leaves that you must crush yourself. Crushed rosemary can be found in the spice section of most supermarkets. McCormick's brand is widely available.

 COOKING TIP:

This soup can be served as soon as it is made, but it improves in flavor when prepared 2 days ahead and "cooked again" or reheated.

Celery Bisque with Stilton Toasts

Celery is one of the winter larder's workhorse vegetables, providing background flavor in hundreds of dishes, but it takes center stage in this creamy, celadon-hued soup. Served with crisp little toasts topped with crumbled Stilton, this simple soup is chic and sophisticated enough to begin a special dinner, but it could just as easily serve as the centerpiece of a casual lunch or supper.

SERVINGS: 4

PREP TIME:
30 minutes

START TO FINISH:
1 hour 20 minutes

MAKE AHEAD:
Yes

BREAD BASKET
CHOICE:
You don't need to offer bread with this soup since it is served with Stilton Toasts.

SOUP-ER SIDE:
Watercress Salad with Red Onion and Chopped Egg Vinaigrette (page 146), omitting the croutons

3   tablespoons unsalted butter

1½ cups chopped leeks, white and light green parts only (about 2 medium leeks)

4   cups sliced celery (from 1 stalk), cut into ¼ inch slices

12 ounces Yukon gold or baking potatoes (about 2 potatoes), peeled and cut into ½-inch dice

4   cups canned low-sodium chicken broth (see tip, facing page)

1   cup crème fraîche, divided (page 23)

2   teaspoons kosher salt, plus more if needed

⅛ to ¼ teaspoon cayenne pepper

1½ tablespoons chopped fresh flat-leaf parsley

Stilton Toasts for serving (facing page)

1. Heat butter in a large, deep-sided pot (with a lid) over medium-high heat. When hot, add leeks and celery and sauté, stirring, for 4 minutes. Add potatoes and broth. Bring mixture to a simmer, then reduce heat. Cook, uncovered, at a simmer until all vegetables are tender, for 20 to 25 minutes.

2. Purée the soup in batches in a food processor, blender, or food mill, and return soup to the pot. (Or use an immersion blender to purée the soup in the pot.) Stir in ⅔ cup of the crème fraîche. Taste soup and season with 2 teaspoons salt and the cayenne pepper. (Soup can be prepared 1 day ahead. Cool, cover, and refrigerate. Reheat over medium heat.)

3. To serve, ladle soup into bowls. Garnish each serving with a dollop or a swirl of the remaining ⅓ cup crème fraîche, sprinkle with parsley, and serve with Stilton Toasts.

Stilton Toasts

MAKES 8 TOASTS

Eight ¼-inch-thick bread slices cut on a sharp diagonal from a baguette
Vegetable oil

2 ½ ounces Stilton cheese or other good-quality blue cheese, crumbled

1 ½ tablespoons crème fraîche (page 23)

2   teaspoons chopped fresh flat-leaf parsley

1. Arrange an oven rack at center position and preheat oven to 350 degrees F. Line a baking sheet with aluminum foil. Brush both sides of the bread slices with oil and arrange on baking sheet. Bake until lightly browned and just crisp, for about 5 minutes per side. Remove and set aside. (Toasts can be prepared 3 hours ahead; leave at cool room temperature.)

2. Preheat oven to 350 degrees F. Use a fork to mix together the crumbled Stilton and crème fraîche in a small bowl. Top each toast with some of the Stilton mixture. Arrange toasts on a baking sheet and bake just until cheese melts, for 2 to 3 minutes. Remove from oven and sprinkle toasts with parsley.

 COOKING TIP:

Because celery is high in sodium, I use canned low-sodium chicken broth in this soup. If you use regular stock, you'll probably want to adjust the amount of added salt; just be sure to season carefully.

Spicy Pork Chili with Cumin Polenta

Pork, not the usual beef or chicken, stars in this robust chili. Cubed pieces of loin are slowly simmered until fork-tender in a beautifully flavored stock piquant with the taste of spicy serrano peppers and brightened with a hit of lime juice. This rich chili is then ladled over mounds of creamy cumin-spiced polenta.

SERVINGS: 6

PREP TIME:
1 hour

START TO FINISH:
2½ to 3 hours

MAKE AHEAD:
Yes

BREAD BASKET
CHOICE:
Crusty peasant loaf

SOUP-ER SIDE:
Best-Ever Greens Salad in Classic Vinaigrette (page 139), made with mixed greens and with sliced avocados and halved cherry tomatoes

CHILI

6   tablespoons vegetable oil, divided, plus more if needed

1½ cups chopped onion

1   cup diced (½-inch dice) carrots

2   tablespoons minced serrano peppers (about 2 peppers; see note, page 72)

3   pounds boneless pork loin, trimmed of all excess fat and cut into 1-inch cubes

½   cup all-purpose flour

1   teaspoon kosher salt, plus more if needed

Freshly ground black pepper

2   tablespoons minced garlic

One 28-ounce can Italian-style plum tomatoes, drained and coarsely chopped

2   tablespoons plus 2 teaspoons fresh lime juice (from about 2 limes)

4   cups low-sodium chicken broth

2   tablespoons chopped fresh cilantro

6   thin lime wedges for garnish (optional)

POLENTA

4   cups chicken stock, plus a little extra if needed

2   teaspoons ground cumin

1   cup yellow cornmeal

1   tablespoon unsalted butter

½   cup whole milk

1. *To make the chili:* Heat 2 tablespoons oil in a large, heavy, deep-sided pot set over medium-high heat. When hot, add onion and carrots and sauté, stirring, for 5 minutes. Add serrano peppers and cook 1 minute more. Remove pan from heat and spoon ingredients onto a plate; set aside. Reserve pot.

2. Put pork in large resealable plastic bag; add flour, 1 teaspoon salt, and several grinds of pepper. Seal bag and shake well to coat pork with flour.

3. Return pot to medium-high heat and add 2 to 3 more tablespoons oil, or enough to coat bottom of pan lightly. When hot, add enough floured pork cubes to fit comfortably in a single layer in pan (do not crowd). Brown pork, turning, for 3 to 4 minutes. Using slotted spoon, transfer pork to paper towels to drain. Repeat with remaining pork, adding more oil as needed.

4. Return all browned pork to pan and add garlic. Cook and toss 1 minute more. Return reserved onion, carrots, and peppers to pan. Add tomatoes, lime juice, and broth. Bring mixture to simmer, then reduce heat. Simmer, uncovered, for 40 minutes, then cover and cook until meat is quite tender, for 50 to 60 minutes more. Taste chili and season with salt and pepper, as needed. (Chili can be prepared 2 days ahead; cool, cover, and refrigerate. Reheat over medium heat.)

continued on next page . . .

…continued

5. *To make the polenta:* Combine 4 cups stock and the cumin in a large, heavy saucepan set over medium-high heat. When stock begins to boil, reduce heat and gradually (in a thin stream) whisk in cornmeal. Cook, stirring constantly, until mixture starts to thicken, for 6 to 8 minutes or less.

6. Stir in butter and milk. Taste and add salt, as needed. (Polenta can be made 2 days ahead; cool, cover, and refrigerate. Reheat over low heat, stirring constantly and adding additional stock, as needed, until polenta is desired texture.)

7. To serve, spoon a generous ½ cup polenta into 6 shallow soup bowls. Ladle pork chili over polenta and sprinkle each portion with some cilantro. Garnish with a lime wedge, if desired.

 AT THE MARKET NOTE:

Serrano peppers are small (1½ inch long) hot peppers with slightly pointed ends. Like many peppers, they start out green and turn red as they mature. Use red ones in this recipe if you can find them. See note about handling hot peppers on page 22.

 COOKING TIP:

I like to use canned low-sodium chicken broth in this recipe to control the salt content: as the chili simmers uncovered for an hour, the salt in the stock will become more concentrated as the liquid reduces.

Tomato, Dill, and White Cheddar Soup

The inspiration for this recipe was a delicious tomato-and-dill soup I ordered one day at a sandwich stand when I first moved to the small New England town where I live. Each time I returned, I would order the soup and try to figure out how it was prepared. After many attempts, I finally came up with a version close to the original. This warm, puréed soup is delicious on its own, but tastes even better when topped with some shaved white Cheddar.

SERVINGS: 6

PREP TIME:
15 minutes

START TO FINISH:
45 minutes

MAKE AHEAD:
Yes

BREAD BASKET CHOICE:
Whole wheat or multi-grain loaf

SOUP-ER SIDE:
Omit bread and serve with Roast Beef and Watercress with Horseradish Cream on Dark Bread (page 151)

2   tablespoons olive oil

3   cups chopped leeks, white and light green parts only (4 to 5 medium leeks)

Four 28-ounce cans diced tomatoes and their juices

4½ cups chicken stock

6   tablespoons chopped fresh dill, plus fresh sprigs for garnish

¼   teaspoon cayenne pepper, plus more if needed

1   teaspoon salt, plus more if needed

½   cup sour cream

One 4-ounce piece sharp white Cheddar cheese, preferably a good farmhouse Cheddar, chilled (see note)

 AT THE MARKET NOTE:
Farmhouse cheddar is an artisanally produced Cheddar cheese. Pale ivory in color, it has a rich, full flavor and a smooth, buttery texture. If not available, use good-quality sharp white Cheddar.

1. Heat olive oil in a large, heavy pot set over medium heat. When hot, add leeks and cook, stirring, until leeks are just softened, for about 3 minutes. Add tomatoes, stock, chopped dill, cayenne, and 1 teaspoon salt, and bring to a simmer. Cook slowly, uncovered, until tomatoes are very soft, for about 20 minutes.

2. Purée the soup in batches in a food processor, blender, or food mill, and return soup to the pot. (Or use an immersion blender to purée the soup in the pot.) Set the pot over low heat; when soup is hot, gradually whisk in the sour cream. Taste soup and season with salt and more cayenne pepper, as needed. (The soup can be prepared 1 day ahead; cool, cover, and refrigerate. Reheat over medium heat.)

3. To serve, ladle soup into 6 shallow soup bowls. Using a vegetable peeler or cheese slicer, shave very thin slices from the piece of Cheddar cheese. Arrange 3 to 4 slices on top of each serving. Garnish each serving with a fresh dill sprig.

Gulf Coast Shrimp Gumbo

This gumbo is a variation on the ones I grew up eating during my childhood in the South. In this version, I use a generous amount of tomatoes and add carrots to the traditional gumbo medley of onions, bell peppers, and celery. Instead of letting okra (that traditional gumbo ingredient) simmer for a long time in the stock, I slice it and sauté it separately, then stir it into the soup at the last minute. Prepared this way, the okra holds its shape and doesn't become stringy. Finally, I employ a quick-cooking method for making roux, the flour-fat mixture (in this recipe, I use vegetable oil) that thickens the gumbo. Served over mounds of white rice, this soup makes a delectable main course. *Laissez les bons temps rouler!*

SERVINGS: 6

PREP TIME:
25 minutes

START TO FINISH:
1 hour

MAKE AHEAD:
Partially

BREAD BASKET
CHOICE:
Crusty baguette

SOUP-ER SIDE:
Best-Ever Greens Salad
in Classic Vinaigrette
(page 139), made with
mixed greens

8	tablespoons vegetable or canola oil, divided
4	tablespoons all-purpose flour
¾	cup chopped onion
¾	cup chopped celery
¾	cup chopped carrot
¾	cup diced, seeded red bell pepper
2 ½	teaspoons minced garlic
¼	teaspoon cayenne pepper
¾	teaspoon dried thyme
⅜	teaspoon kosher salt, plus more if needed
⅜	teaspoon freshly ground black pepper, plus more if needed
3	cups chicken stock, plus extra if needed
One 28-ounce can diced tomatoes, drained well	
5	fresh flat-leaf parsley sprigs
2	bay leaves, broken in half
12	ounces okra, cut into ¼-inch rounds
6	ounces andouille sausage, cut into ¼-inch dice
1	pound large uncooked shrimp, shelled and deveined
4	cups cooked white rice

1. To make roux, heat 4 tablespoons oil in a medium, heavy skillet set over medium heat. When hot, add flour and stir constantly with a wooden spoon until the mixture thickens and turns deep reddish brown, for 6 to 8 minutes. Remove from heat and set aside.

2. Add 2 tablespoons oil to a large, heavy, deep-sided pot set over medium-high heat. When hot, add onion, celery, carrot, and red bell pepper. Sauté, stirring constantly, for 3 minutes. Add garlic and cook, stirring, for 1 minute more. Stir in cayenne pepper, thyme, ⅜ teaspoon salt, and ⅜ teaspoon black pepper. Add stock, tomatoes, parsley sprigs, and bay leaves, and bring mixture to a simmer. Reduce heat to low so that mixture stays at simmer, then whisk in reserved roux.

3. Simmer gumbo until vegetables are tender and mixture has thickened, for about 20 minutes.

4. While gumbo is simmering, cook the okra. Heat the remaining 2 tablespoons oil in a large, heavy skillet set over medium-high heat. When hot, add okra and sauté, stirring, until just lightly browned around the edges, for 4 to 5 minutes. Add okra and sausage to the gumbo after it has simmered for 20 minutes. Cook for 1 minute to heat through. (Gumbo can be prepared to this point 1 day ahead; cool, cover, and refrigerate. Reheat over medium heat and proceed with recipe.)

5. When ready to serve, add shrimp to the gumbo and cook until the shrimp curl and turn pink, for about 3 minutes. Do not overcook or shrimp will be tough. Taste gumbo and season with salt and pepper, as needed. If soup is too thick, thin it with extra stock to desired consistency.

6. To serve, place about ⅔ cup rice in 6 shallow soup bowls and ladle gumbo over rice.

Fennel × Two Soup

Fennel is one of my favorite vegetables, and once I discovered it, I became a real aficionado. Here, I use two forms of fennel to amplify its sweet anise flavor. First, I sauté chopped fresh fennel, then I simmer crushed fennel seeds in a little cream, which is swirled into the finished soup, infusing it with even more fennel flavor.

SERVINGS: 8

PREP TIME:
20 minutes

START TO FINISH:
1 hour 10 minutes

MAKE AHEAD:
Yes

BREAD BASKET CHOICE:
Crusty sourdough or ciabatta

SOUP-ER SIDE:
Watercress Salad with Red Onion and Chopped Egg Vinaigrette (page 146), or omit bread and serve with Vegetable Pitas with Goat Cheese and Fresh Herbs (page 152)

4	large fennel bulbs
2	tablespoons olive oil
2	medium onions, chopped
8	ounces (about 1 medium) white-skinned potato, peeled and diced
1	teaspoon kosher salt, plus more if needed
½	teaspoon freshly ground black pepper, plus more if needed
4	cups chicken stock, plus more if needed
2	teaspoons fresh lemon juice, plus more if needed
1	cup whipping cream
¾	teaspoon dried tarragon
1	teaspoon fennel seeds, crushed (see tip)

 COOKING TIP:

You can crush fennel seeds in an electric spice grinder, or place in a mortar and crush finely with a pestle, or seal them in a plastic bag and pound with a meat mallet or rolling pin. The seeds should be finely crushed.

1. Cut off stalks from fennel (if attached) and reserve feathery tops for garnish. (Reserve tops in a glass of water to prevent wilting.) Halve the fennel bulbs lengthwise and cut out and discard the tough inner cores. Chop enough fennel to yield 6 cups.

2. Heat oil in a large, heavy pot (with a lid) set over medium-high heat. When hot, add chopped fennel, onion, potato, 1 teaspoon salt, and ½ teaspoon pepper. Sauté, stirring, until vegetables are slightly softened, for about 5 minutes. Add 4 cups stock and 2 teaspoons lemon juice. Bring mixture to a simmer, then reduce heat and cover. Cook at a simmer until vegetables are tender, for about 30 minutes.

3. While soup is cooking, combine cream, tarragon, and crushed fennel seeds in a small saucepan and simmer for 5 minutes. Remove from heat and let sit for 10 minutes to allow the flavors of the fennel and tarragon to infuse into the cream.

4. Purée the soup in batches in a food processor, blender, or food mill, and return soup to the pot. (Or use an immersion blender to purée the soup in the pot.) Whisk in fennel-infused cream. Taste soup and season with salt and pepper, and add more lemon juice to taste, if needed. If soup is too thick, thin with extra chicken stock. (The soup can be made 1 day ahead; cool, cover, and refrigerate. Reheat over medium heat.)

5. To serve, ladle soup into 8 shallow soup bowls and place 1 or 2 feathery fennel sprigs in the center of each serving.

Mama Veli's Pozole

Pozole (also spelled posole) is the Spanish word for hominy—large dried corn kernels with the hull and germ removed. Both the hominy and this traditional Mexican Christmas soup in which it is used share the same name. There are many variations of pozole, but the following is a personal favorite. The handwritten recipe was given to me by my friend Elinor Lipman, a talented novelist and gifted cook who fell in love with this special pozole one Christmas Eve at an open house hosted by Martha and Juan Perea. Martha is the daughter of the soup's source—Mama Veli! Like most pozole soups, this one is served with an array of colorful fresh garnishes. Bowls of sliced radishes, cubed avocado, shredded cabbage, chopped cilantro, chopped onion, and lime wedges are set on the table for diners to add as they like.

SERVINGS: 6

PREP TIME:
1 hour

START TO FINISH:
1 hour 50 minutes

MAKE AHEAD:
Partially

BREAD BASKET
CHOICE:
You could offer some warm tortillas with the soup if you like, but the colorful garnishes will probably suffice on their own.

SOUP-ER SIDE:
Red, Yellow, and Orange Pepper Salad with Tequila-Lime Dressing (page 148)

4	cups chicken stock, plus extra if needed
2	skinless, boneless chicken breast halves (10 to 12 ounces total boneless)
12	ounces (about 10) tomatillos
1	cup chopped onion
¾	cup small cilantro sprigs
5	large garlic cloves, peeled
One 3-inch jalapeño pepper, stemmed and quartered lengthwise, including seeds (see tip)	
Two 15-ounce cans hominy (posole), drained (see note)	
½	teaspoon dried oregano
Kosher salt	

GARNISHES

½	cup halved, thinly sliced radishes
½	cup cubed avocado tossed in 1 teaspoon fresh lime juice
½	cup shredded cabbage
¼	cup chopped fresh cilantro
½	cup chopped onion
6	thin lime slices

1. Bring 4 cups chicken stock to a boil in a large, heavy saucepan (with a lid). Add chicken breasts, cover, and simmer until cooked through, for about 14 minutes or longer. Using tongs or a slotted spoon, transfer chicken to plate. Reserve poaching liquid. You should have 3 cups liquid; if not, add enough stock to equal this amount. Shred the chicken and set aside. (Soup can be prepared to this point 1 day ahead; see tip on page 78. Cover poaching liquid and chicken separately and refrigerate.)

continued on next page…

…continued

2. Remove and discard husks from the tomatillos; rinse and coarsely chop. Put chopped tomatillos in a large bowl; add onion, cilantro, garlic, and jalapeño. In a food processor or blender, process half of this mixture with ½ cup water until chunky; repeat with remaining half and another ½ cup water.

3. Place the tomatillo mixture in a large, deep-sided pot. Add the reserved chicken poaching liquid, shredded chicken, hominy, and oregano. Bring mixture to a simmer and cook just until all ingredients are heated through, for 2 to 3 minutes. Taste soup and season with salt, as needed.

4. To serve, ladle soup into 6 soup bowls. Arrange garnishes in small bowls and pass separately.

 AT THE MARKET NOTE:

Canned hominy is sold in white or yellow varieties; either works fine in this recipe. Goya brand hominy is widely available in supermarkets.

 COOKING TIPS:

When you use a whole jalapeño with its seeds, the soup will be quite spicy (the seeds and pithy membrane contribute much of the heat). For less heat, use only half or even one quarter of the seeds, according to your taste. See note about handling hot peppers on page 22.

The soup is prettiest when served immediately. (Its bright green color darkens when it sits longer, but it still tastes delicious.)

Black Bean Soup with a Hint of Orange

What makes this black bean soup different from classic versions is its refreshing orange accent. Both orange juice and zest lend a clean, bright note to the rich, dark beans. I employ the quick method for soaking them—just an hour in hot water—and prep the other ingredients during this short wait.

SERVINGS: 6

PREP TIME:
10 minutes, plus 1 hour
for soaking the beans

START TO FINISH:
1½ hours, plus 1 hour
for soaking the beans

MAKE AHEAD:
Yes

**BREAD BASKET
CHOICE:**
Cornbread or
tortilla chips

SOUP-ER SIDE:
Red, Yellow, and Orange
Pepper Salad with
Tequila-Lime Dressing
(page 148)

1	pound dried black beans
2	tablespoons olive oil
8	ounces Spanish chorizo sausage, cut into ¼-inch cubes (see note)
2	cups chopped onion
1½	tablespoons dried oregano
⅛	teaspoon red pepper flakes
½	teaspoon kosher salt, plus more if needed
7 to 8	cups chicken stock
1	cup fresh orange juice
⅓	cup sour cream
2	teaspoons very finely julienned orange zest
2	tablespoons chopped cilantro for garnish

 AT THE MARKET NOTE:

Chorizo is a highly seasoned pork sausage available in both Spanish and Mexican varieties. For this recipe, use the firmer smoked Spanish type, which is made with pork that is already cooked. (Mexican chorizo is prepared with fresh pork enclosed in a casing.) Chorizo is available at Spanish markets, specialty food stores, and some supermarkets, such as Whole Foods.

1. Rinse and sort through the beans to remove any pebbles. Put beans in a large heatproof bowl and cover with 6 cups boiling water. Soak beans for 1 hour, then drain and set aside.

2. Heat oil in a large, heavy, deep-sided pot (with a lid) set over medium heat. When hot, add chorizo and sauté, stirring, for 3 minutes. Add onion and cook, stirring, for 3 minutes more. Add oregano, red pepper flakes, and ½ teaspoon salt. Cook and stir for 1 minute more. Add beans and 7 cups stock and bring mixture to a simmer. Reduce heat and cover.

3. Cook soup, covered, at a simmer until beans are tender, for about 1 hour or longer. Remove lid, and if too much liquid has evaporated, add up to 1 cup of the remaining stock. If the soup seems too thin, remove ½ cup of solids from the soup and purée them in a food processor or blender, then stir them into the soup to thicken it. Add the orange juice to the soup.

4. Taste soup and season with salt, as needed. (The soup can be made 2 days ahead; cool, cover, and refrigerate. Reheat, uncovered, over low heat.)

5. To serve, divide soup among 6 soup bowls. Garnish the center of each serving with a scant tablespoon of sour cream, then sprinkle each with some julienned orange zest and chopped cilantro.

Russian Vegetable Soup

Don't be put off by the list of very humble ingredients in this recipe. Several of the testers for this cookbook told me that when they first looked at the recipe they were convinced that it would be "rather ordinary." They were surprised and delighted by the glorious flavors these winter root vegetables produced after being simmered together slowly for a couple of hours. Generous dollops of sour cream and a shower of chopped fresh dill make delicious garnishes. Another bonus: This soup tastes even better when made a day in advance.

SERVINGS: 6

PREP TIME:
15 to 20 minutes

START TO FINISH:
2½ hours

MAKE AHEAD:
Yes

BREAD BASKET
CHOICE:
Pumpernickel, crusty peasant loaf, or sourdough

SOUP-ER SIDE:
Best-Ever Greens Salad in Classic Vinaigrette (page 139), with sliced cucumbers added

One 2-pound cabbage, halved lengthwise, cored, and cut into 1-inch-thick wedges

2 medium carrots, peeled and cut into ¼-inch-thick slices

2 ribs celery, cut into ½-inch-thick slices

3 medium turnips (12 ounces), peeled and cut into 1-inch cubes

8 cups beef stock, divided

One 6-ounce can tomato paste

1 teaspoon kosher salt, plus more if needed

Freshly ground black pepper

3 tablespoons vegetable oil

2 medium onions, peeled, halved lengthwise, and cut into ¼-inch-thick slices

1 large garlic clove, finely chopped

1 large russet potato (12 ounces), peeled and cut into 1-inch cubes

1 cup sour cream

⅓ cup chopped fresh dill

1. Put the cabbage, carrots, celery, turnips, and 6 cups of the stock in a large, deep stockpot. Bring to a simmer, then stir in the tomato paste, 1 teaspoon salt, and several grinds of pepper. Simmer, uncovered, until the vegetables are very tender, for about 1½ hours.

2. Meanwhile, heat the oil in a medium, heavy skillet. When hot, add the onions and sauté until softened, for 3 to 4 minutes. Add the garlic and sauté for 1 minute more. Remove from heat and set aside.

3. When the vegetables in the stockpot have simmered for 1½ hours, add the onion mixture and the cubed potatoes. Add the remaining 2 cups stock, and if there isn't enough liquid to cover the vegetables, add 1 to 2 cups water to cover them. Simmer until the potatoes are just tender, for another 30 minutes. Taste soup and season with salt, as needed. (The soup can be prepared to this point 2 days ahead and will improve in flavor. Cool, cover, and refrigerate, then reheat over medium heat.)

4. Serve the soup in a large tureen or in individual bowls. Garnish each serving with a large dollop of sour cream, and sprinkle chopped dill on top.

"Melt in Your Mouth" Beef and Barley Soup

My friend Elisabeth Lubin, a talented cook and hostess, says that of all the dishes she has made for her family over the years, this soup is the recipe they request most, especially during the cold days of winter. Its great flavor comes from long, slow cooking. Pieces of beef chuck are sautéed and simmered in stock, then combined with vegetables and barley and cooked even longer. The result is fork-tender meat and vegetables that seem to melt in your mouth, as the title indicates.

SERVINGS: 8

PREP TIME:
45 minutes

START TO FINISH:
3 hours

MAKE AHEAD:
Yes

BREAD BASKET
CHOICE:
Crusty peasant loaf or
sourdough

SOUP-ER SIDE:
Best-Ever Greens Salad
in Classic Vinaigrette
(page 139), made with
mixed greens

4 to 4 ½ pounds boneless beef chuck, trimmed of excess fat, cut into 1-inch pieces

9 to 10 tablespoons olive oil, plus more for sautéing meat

8 cups beef stock, plus a little extra if needed

1 ½ teaspoons Worcestershire sauce

1 teaspoon soy sauce

1 teaspoon kosher salt, plus more if needed

Freshly ground black pepper

3 medium carrots, peeled, halved, and cut into ¼-inch-thick slices

3 ribs celery, halved and cut into ¼-inch-thick slices

2 medium parsnips, peeled, halved and cut into ¼-inch-thick slices

1 medium onion, coarsely chopped

8 ounces sliced white mushrooms

1 large Yukon gold potato, peeled and cut into ½-inch cubes

1 cup pearl barley

1 teaspoon crushed dried thyme

2 tablespoons chopped fresh flat-leaf parsley for garnish (optional)

1. Pat meat dry with paper towels. Line a large plate or platter with a double thickness of paper towels.

2. Pour enough oil into a large, deep-sided pot (with a lid) to coat the bottom (4 to 5 tablespoons). Set the pot over medium-high heat. When oil is hot but not smoking, add enough pieces of meat to fit comfortably in a single layer (do not crowd). Brown the meat on all sides, turning often, for 4 to 5 minutes. Using a slotted spoon, transfer meat to paper towels to drain. Repeat with remaining meat, adding more oil if needed.

3. Remove pot from heat and wipe out any excess oil with a paper towel. Return meat to pan and add beef stock, Worcestershire sauce, soy sauce, 1 teaspoon salt, and several grinds of pepper. Bring to a simmer over medium-high heat, then reduce heat and cover. Cook at a simmer for 1 ½ hours.

4. While the meat is cooking, heat 3 tablespoons oil in a large, heavy skillet over medium-high heat. When hot, add the carrots, celery, parsnips, and onion and sauté until just slightly softened, for about 5 minutes. Remove skillet from heat and set aside.

5. Heat 2 tablespoons oil in a medium skillet set over medium-high heat. When hot, add the mushrooms, and sauté, turning and adding more oil as needed, until lightly browned, for 4 to 5 minutes. Set aside.

6. After the meat has cooked for 1½ hours, add the sautéed vegetables (but not the mushrooms), cubed potato, barley, and thyme to the pot. Bring mixture to a simmer, cover, and cook until barley and meat are tender, for 45 to 60 minutes. Stir occasionally, adding more water if consistency becomes too thick. Add the sautéed mushrooms to the soup and simmer until heated through, for 2 to 3 minutes. Taste soup and season with salt and pepper, as needed. Total cooking time will be about 2½ hours. (Soup can be prepared 2 days ahead; cool, cover, and refrigerate. Reheat over medium heat.)

7. To serve, ladle soup into soup bowls and garnish with chopped parsley, if desired.

 COOKING TIP:

This soup improves in flavor when made in advance, but it will thicken considerably as it sits. Thin it with additional water, and season with more salt and pepper, as needed. If you make the soup ahead and refrigerate it, excess fat from the beef will collect on the surface and solidify. It's easy to simply spoon it off, but be sure to leave a little, as it will add to the depth of flavor.

4 Spring

MARCH | APRIL | MAY

Just as the blanket of snow recedes, chives make a faint appearance in my garden. Only a few inches tall, they signal new possibilities in the kitchen. They mark the beginning of all things green to come. Soon, the farmers' markets will be filled with sleek stalks of asparagus, young sweet peas, bunches of peppery watercress, tender new lettuces, and bouquets of parsley and mint—filling the spring soup pot with fresh, delicious flavors.

All of these greens make starring appearances in this chapter. Heavenly Asparagus Soup with Tarragon Cream and Sweet Pea Soup with Early Chives burst with verdancy and flavor. Penne, Asparagus, and Peas in Parmesan Broth and Primavera Vegetable Soup in a Lemon Broth showcase spring's fresh cornucopia with delicately scented broths. Paella Soup and Spring Risotto Soup are fresh takes on traditional entrées. With its golden saffron hue, creamy paella soup is a showstopper, while risotto *zuppa* is light and vibrant, perfect for the season.

My New England neighbors, many of whom hole up for the winter, begin to roll out the welcome mat come spring. The social season officially begins with St. Patrick's Day, and for that festive occasion—when it is often still chilly out—you'll find a recipe for a satisfying corned beef and cabbage soup baked under a tender crust. For Easter, begin your celebration with Dreamy Creamy Artichoke Soup or Carrot Soup Scented with Sesame and Chives. And, for midday get-togethers or light suppers, try Emily's Springtime Salmon Chowder.

Like the season itself, spring soups are filled with promise—fresh new beginnings in the garden and at the table.

Heavenly Asparagus Soup with Tarragon Cream

Spring's most celebrated crop is the main ingredient in this creamy "celestial" creation. Instead of potatoes, rice is used to thicken the soup, and a sprinkle of cayenne pepper adds a subtle hint of heat. Dollops of crème fraîche, scented with tarragon, make a tempting garnish.

SERVINGS: 4

PREP TIME:
15 minutes

START TO FINISH:
50 minutes

MAKE AHEAD:
Yes

BREAD BASKET
CHOICE:
Crusty baguette, ciabatta, or sourdough loaf

SOUP-ER SIDE:
Watercress Salad
with Red Onion
and Chopped Egg
Vinaigrette (page 146),
or omit bread and serve
with Crab and Avocado
Sandwiches (page 155)
or Vegetable Pitas with
Goat Cheese and Fresh
Herbs (page 152)

1½ pounds medium asparagus

2   tablespoons unsalted butter

½   cup chopped shallots

4   cups chicken stock, plus a little extra if needed

½   teaspoon kosher salt, plus more if needed

Scant ⅛ teaspoon cayenne pepper

⅓   cup long-grain white rice, uncooked

½   cup crème fraîche (page 23)

1½ tablespoons chopped fresh tarragon, plus several sprigs for garnish

1. Cut off and discard tough bases from asparagus. Cut spears into ½-inch-thick pieces.

2. Heat butter in a large, heavy pot (with a lid) set over medium-high heat, until hot. Add shallots and cook, stirring, until softened, for about 2 minutes. Add asparagus slices and cook, stirring, 1 minute more. Add stock, ½ teaspoon salt, cayenne pepper, and rice. Bring mixture to a simmer, then reduce heat, cover pot, and cook until vegetables are completely tender, for about 20 minutes.

3. Purée the soup in batches in a food processor, blender, or food mill, and return soup to the pot. (Or use an immersion blender to purée the soup in the pot.) Place the crème fraîche in a small bowl and stir in the chopped tarragon. Whisk ⅓ cup of the tarragon crème fraîche, a little at a time, into the soup. Save the remaining crème fraîche for the garnish.

4. Taste soup and season with salt, as needed. If soup is too thick, thin it with a few tablespoons of extra stock. (The soup can be prepared 1 day ahead. Cool, cover, and refrigerate. Reheat over medium heat.)

5. To serve, ladle the soup into 4 soup bowls. Garnish each serving with a dollop of the tarragon crème fraîche and a tarragon sprig.

Cream of Parsley Soup

During a trip to Burgundy several years ago, I was stunned by the creativity of the region's chefs. At Hostellerie de Levernois, just outside the town of Beaune, a delicious soup caught my eye and my palate. At first, I couldn't discern what the flavoring was. Finally, a knowledgeable waiter revealed that parsley was the prime ingredient. I never would have thought of using this commonplace herb in such an inventive way.

SERVINGS: 4

PREP TIME:
30 minutes

START TO FINISH:
1 hour

MAKE AHEAD:
Yes

BREAD BASKET CHOICE:
Crusty baguette or sourdough loaf

SOUP-ER SIDE:
Green Bean, Cherry Tomato, and Bacon Salad (page 143), or omit bread and serve with All-Time Favorite Egg Salad and Olive Sandwiches (page 156) or Vegetable Pitas with Goat Cheese and Fresh Herbs (page 152)

---

2 to 3 large bunches fresh flat-leaf parsley (enough to make 3 cups of leaves and tender stems)

2 tablespoons unsalted butter

2 cups chopped leeks, white and light green parts only (about 3 medium leeks)

2½ cups chicken stock

1½ cups light cream

8 ounces all-purpose potatoes, peeled and cut into ½-inch dice

1 teaspoon kosher salt, plus more if needed

⅛ teaspoon white pepper

2 to 3 teaspoons fresh lemon juice (optional)

 COOKING TIPS:

This soup is prettiest when served immediately; its bright green color will darken as it sits.

This soup is also good chilled. If serving it cold, you may need to thin it slightly with extra stock or cream. You will probably need to season it with extra salt, as well.

---

1. Rinse parsley well and dry with paper towels or clean kitchen towels. Remove enough sprigs and tender stems to make 3 cups well-packed parsley.

2. Heat butter in a medium, nonreactive heavy pot (with a lid) over medium heat. When hot, add leeks and cook, stirring, until softened, for about 4 minutes.

3. Add stock, cream, and potatoes to the pot. Bring the mixture to a simmer, then cover, reduce heat, and cook at a simmer until potatoes are tender, for about 20 minutes. (Do not let the soup come to a boil.) Add the parsley sprigs and cook for 1 to 2 minutes longer.

4. Purée the soup in batches in a food processor, blender, or food mill, and return the soup to the pot. (Or use an immersion blender to purée the soup in the pot.) Season with 1 teaspoon salt (or more to taste) and the white pepper. Taste soup, and if you want to add a refreshing accent, add up to 3 teaspoons lemon juice. (Soup can be prepared 1 day ahead; cool, cover, and refrigerate. Reheat over medium heat.)

5. To serve, ladle into 4 soup bowls and serve immediately.

Primavera Vegetable Soup in a Lemon Broth

Primavera means "spring" in Italian, and this recipe showcases a veritable garden of this season's colorful vegetables, accented with lemon and served simply in a rich, clear broth. The secret to making this soup is to use very good quality chicken stock. If time permits, prepare it with the Made-from-Scratch Chicken Stock. If you're in a rush, don't hesitate to try the Shortcut Chicken Stock, which also works beautifully.

SERVINGS: 4

PREP TIME:
15 minutes

START TO FINISH:
1 hour

MAKE AHEAD:
No

BREAD BASKET CHOICE:
Grissini (Italian bread sticks) or ciabatta

SOUP-ER SIDE:
Watercress Salad with Red Onion and Chopped Egg Vinaigrette (page 146)

1	medium fennel bulb
6	cups Made-from-Scratch Chicken Stock (page 16) or Shortcut Chicken Stock (page 20)
1½	tablespoons fresh lemon juice
1½	teaspoons chopped fresh thyme
3	medium carrots, peeled and cut on the diagonal into ¼-inch-thick pieces
2	small white turnips, peeled, quartered, and cut into ¼-inch-thick slices
3	ounces haricots verts or tender young green beans, ends trimmed and beans cut into 1-inch pieces
4	green onions, including 2 inches of green tops, cut into 1-inch pieces
5 to 6	ounces very thin asparagus, tough ends snapped off and stalks cut on diagonal into 1-inch pieces
1½	teaspoons lemon zest
	Kosher salt

1. Cut off and discard stalks (if attached) from fennel. Halve the bulb lengthwise and cut out and discard the tough inner core; cut the fennel into thin julienne strips.

2. Bring stock to a simmer in a large, nonreactive pot set over medium-high heat. When hot, add lemon juice and thyme.

3. Add fennel, carrots, and turnips; return to a simmer and cook for 3 minutes. Add haricots verts, green onions, and asparagus; bring to simmer again and cook for 3 minutes, or slightly longer until vegetables are tender.

4. Stir in lemon zest. Taste soup and season with salt, if needed. Ladle soup into 4 soup bowls and serve immediately.

Spring New Potato and Garlic Soup

So quick, so easy, so chic! That's how I describe this enticing soup made with just a handful of ingredients. The garlic flavor comes from Boursin, a creamy garlic-and-herb-scented French cheese. Broken into small pieces and melted in warm half-and-half, it forms the base of the soup. Thinly sliced parboiled new potatoes are stirred into the silken-smooth cheese mixture and fresh herbs are added as a garnish. The servings are on the small side because this potage is rich, but you could easily double the recipe if you like.

SERVINGS: 4

PREP TIME:
10 minutes

START TO FINISH:
25 minutes

MAKE AHEAD:
No

BREAD BASKET CHOICE:
Crusty baguette

SOUP-ER SIDE:
Best-Ever Greens Salad in Classic Vinaigrette (page 139), made with mixed greens

12 ounces small new red-skin potatoes (1 to 1½ inches in diameter), scrubbed but not peeled

2 teaspoons kosher salt, plus more if needed

2 cups half-and-half

One 5-ounce package Boursin cheese with garlic and herbs, broken into small pieces (see note)

Ground white pepper

4 teaspoons chopped fresh flat-leaf parsley, plus a few extra sprigs for garnish

4 teaspoons chopped fresh chives, plus a few whole chives for garnish

AT THE MARKET NOTE:
There are several brands of garlic-and-herb-scented cheeses, but for this soup, Boursin with Garlic and Fine Herbs is the best choice. It is available in the cheese section of many supermarkets.

1. Halve the potatoes and cut into slices that are ⅛ inch thick or less. Bring a large, heavy saucepan of water to a boil. Add potatoes and 2 teaspoons salt. Cook until potatoes are tender when pierced with a knife, for about 5 to 6 minutes after water returns to a boil. Drain potatoes and set aside.

2. Add the half-and-half and Boursin to the same saucepan. Set the pan over medium-low heat and stir until cheese melts, for about 3 to 4 minutes. Be careful not to let the mixture come to a boil.

3. Add the cooked potatoes to the half-and-half mixture and cook just until warmed through, for 1 to 2 minutes. Taste soup and season with salt and white pepper, as needed.

4. To serve, ladle soup into 4 soup bowls and garnish each serving with a generous sprinkling of chopped parsley and chives. For extra visual pizzazz, top each portion with a couple of parsley sprigs and a few long whole chives, if desired.

Carrot Soup Scented with Sesame and Chives

A mixture of sautéed carrots, leeks, and celery is cooked in stock, puréed, and seasoned with a splash of toasted sesame oil. What makes this soup extra special, however, is the garnish. Each serving is topped with golden croutons, toasted sesame seeds, and snipped chives, then drizzled with a little more sesame oil.

SERVINGS: 6

PREP TIME:
15 minutes

START TO FINISH:
45 to 50 minutes

MAKE AHEAD:
Yes

BREAD BASKET
CHOICE:
You don't need to offer bread with this soup since it is garnished with golden croutons.

SOUP-ER SIDE:
Best-Ever Greens Salad in Classic Vinaigrette (page 139), made with baby romaine or mixed greens

4 ½ tablespoons unsalted butter, divided

3 ½ cups (about 1 ½ pounds) peeled, diced carrots

1   cup chopped leeks, white and light green parts only (1 to 2 medium leeks)

½   cup chopped celery

6   cups chicken stock

1   teaspoon kosher salt, plus more if needed

½   cup light cream or half-and-half

½   cup sour cream

3   teaspoons Asian sesame oil, divided (see note)

2   cups bread cubes (¾-inch dice) cut from day-old bread, preferably a French country loaf with crusts removed

2   tablespoons sesame seeds

2   tablespoons chopped fresh chives

AT THE MARKET NOTE:

Sesame oil is available in light and dark varieties. For this recipe, be sure to use a dark sesame oil, also called Asian or Oriental sesame oil. You'll find it in the Asian foods section of most supermarkets.

1. Heat 2 ½ tablespoons of the butter in a large, heavy, deep-sided pot set over medium heat. When hot, add carrots, leeks, and celery and cook, stirring often, until vegetables are softened, for about 10 minutes. Add stock and 1 teaspoon salt. Bring mixture to a simmer, reduce heat, and cook at a simmer until the vegetables are tender, for about 30 minutes.

2. Purée the soup in batches in a food processor, blender, or food mill, and return soup to the pot. (Or use an immersion blender to purée the soup in the pot.) Gradually whisk in the cream, then the sour cream. Stir in 1 ½ teaspoons of the sesame oil. Taste soup and season with salt, as needed. (Soup can be prepared 1 day ahead; cool, cover, and refrigerate. Reheat over medium heat.)

3. For garnish, heat the remaining 2 tablespoons butter in a medium, heavy skillet set over medium-high heat. When hot, add bread cubes and cook, tossing, until golden brown and crispy, for 3 to 4 minutes. Remove bread cubes and set aside. In the same skillet, add sesame seeds and stir constantly over medium-high heat until they turn a rich golden brown, for 4 to 5 minutes or less, watching carefully to prevent burning. Transfer sesame seeds to small bowl. (Bread cubes and sesame seeds can be prepared 4 hours ahead and left at room temperature. Cover bread cubes loosely with foil and leave seeds uncovered.)

4. To serve, ladle soup into 6 shallow soup bowls. Mound toasted bread croutons in center of each serving and sprinkle with sesame seeds and chives, then drizzle some of remaining 1 ½ teaspoons sesame oil over.

Dreamy Creamy Artichoke Soup

When I began giving cooking classes back in the 1970s, this was one of the first soup recipes I taught to my students. It's still popular today for the same reasons it was then: it's simple to prepare, doesn't call for many ingredients, and the flavor is sublime.

SERVINGS: 6

PREP TIME:
10 minutes

START TO FINISH:
45 minutes

MAKE AHEAD:
Yes

**BREAD BASKET
CHOICE:**
Crusty baguette or
ciabatta

SOUP-ER SIDE:
Watercress Salad
with Red Onion
and Chopped Egg
Vinaigrette (page 146)

4	tablespoons unsalted butter
2	cups chopped leeks, white and light green parts only (about 3 medium leeks)
4	cups (18 to 20 ounces) frozen artichoke hearts, thawed and patted dry
5	cups chicken stock
1¼	cups heavy or whipping cream
6	tablespoons grated Parmesan cheese, preferably Parmigiano-Reggiano

Kosher salt

Ground white pepper

1½ tablespoons chopped fresh chives or flat-leaf parsley

1. Melt the butter in a large, heavy pot over medium heat. Add the leeks and cook, stirring, until softened, for 3 to 4 minutes. Add the artichoke hearts and cook, stirring, for 2 minutes more. Add the stock and bring mixture to a simmer. Cook, uncovered, until the leeks and artichoke hearts are tender, for about 25 minutes.

2. Purée the soup in batches in a food processor, blender, or food mill, and return soup to the pot. (Or use an immersion blender to purée the soup in the pot.) Whisk in ¾ cup of the cream and 4 tablespoons of the Parmesan. Taste soup and season with salt and white pepper. (Soup can be prepared 1 day ahead; cool, cover, and refrigerate. Reheat over medium heat.)

3. For the garnish, whip the remaining ½ cup cream until just firm. Whisk in the remaining 2 tablespoons Parmesan.

4. To serve, ladle the soup into 6 soup bowls and top each serving with a dollop of the Parmesan cream (which will start to melt immediately). Sprinkle each serving with chives or parsley.

Spring Risotto Soup

Risotto takes center stage in this soup. It is seasoned simply with Parmesan, then mounded in the middle of shallow soup bowls and surrounded by a delicious chicken broth studded with spring vegetables. Both the risotto and the broth can be made a day ahead, so that at serving time you need only to reheat each and cook some spring vegetables in the simmering stock.

SERVINGS: 4

PREP TIME:
15 minutes

START TO FINISH:
45 minutes

MAKE AHEAD:
Partially

BREAD BASKET
CHOICE:
Ciabatta

SOUP-ER SIDE:
Arugula Salad Tossed
with Parmesan Oil and
Lemon (page 140)

8 cups good chicken stock, preferably Made-from-Scratch Chicken Stock (page 16) or Shortcut Chicken Stock (page 20), divided

2 tablespoons unsalted butter

½ cup minced shallots

1 cup Arborio rice

3 tablespoons grated Parmesan cheese, preferably Parmigiano-Reggiano, plus shaved Parmesan for the garnish (see tip, page 96)

Kosher salt

4 ounces cremini mushrooms, rinsed, dried, and sliced very thinly through the stems (see note, page 96)

2 to 3 ounces sugar snap peas, cut on the diagonal into thin slices

¾ cup thinly sliced (on the diagonal) green onions, including 2 inches of green tops

Fleur de sel (French sea salt), optional

1. Place 3½ cups of the stock in a medium, heavy saucepan over medium-low heat and bring to a simmer. (Keep remaining stock covered and refrigerated.) Reduce heat and keep at a gentle simmer.

2. Heat butter in a medium, heavy saucepan over medium-low heat. When melted, add the shallots and sauté until softened and translucent, for 2 to 3 minutes. Add the rice and stir for 1 minute until coated and opaque. Add ½ cup simmering stock and cook, stirring constantly with a wooden spoon, until all liquid has been absorbed.

3. Continue adding stock in ½ cup amounts, stirring constantly and making certain that each addition is completely absorbed before adding the next. It is important to stir the rice so that it does not stick. When done, the rice should be tender, but slightly chewy. Total cooking time should be 20 to 25 minutes. (If you have a little stock left over after making the risotto, add it to the reserved stock.) Stir in the grated Parmesan. Taste rice and season with salt, as needed. (The risotto can be prepared 1 day ahead. Spread the warm risotto in an even layer on a baking sheet lined with plastic. Cool to room temperature, cover, and refrigerate. To reheat, combine ⅓ cup stock with risotto in a saucepan set over medium heat. Stir constantly until warm.)

continued on next page...

...continued

4. When ready to serve soup, bring the remaining stock in sauce-pan to a simmer, and add the mushrooms, sugar snap peas, and green onions. Cook until tender, for 2 to 3 minutes.

5. Divide the risotto evenly and mound it in the center of 4 large shallow soup bowls (see tip). Ladle the broth around the risotto in each bowl. Garnish each serving with some shaved Parmesan. If desired, sprinkle a little fleur de sel over each serving.

 AT THE MARKET NOTE:

Cremini mushrooms are also packaged as baby bellas (when fully matured, cremini mushrooms are portobellos) or brown mushrooms.

 COOKING TIPS:

You can vary the vegetables for this soup. For example, try slim asparagus or snow peas sliced on the diagonal, or add some fresh or frozen peas to the mix. Just make certain that the vegetables you use will cook quickly (2 to 3 minutes).

An attractive and easy way to mound risotto in the soup bowls is to pack it into a ½-cup ramekin. Run a sharp knife around the edges of the ramekin to loosen, then unmold the risotto in the center of a soup bowl. The risotto will hold its shape nicely.

To make Parmesan shavings, use a cheese slicer or vegetable peeler to shave thin strips from a 3- to 4-ounce piece of Parmesan cheese. (For best results, bring cheese to room temperature before making Parmesan shavings.)

"Just Greens" Soup

A surprising mélange of vegetables combines to make this very savory soup. Savoy cabbage adds a big, assertive flavor, while snow peas and green onions contribute milder notes. These vegetables are simmered quickly in good stock so that they retain their verdant color as well as a little crunch. Bits of sautéed bacon and a sprinkle of parsley make good garnishes for this light yet satisfying potage.

SERVINGS: 4

PREP TIME:
30 minutes

START TO FINISH:
1 hour

MAKE AHEAD:
Partially

BREAD BASKET CHOICE:
Crusty peasant loaf or ciabatta

SOUP-ER SIDE:
Omit bread and serve with All-Time Favorite Egg Salad and Olive Sandwiches (page 156)

4   bacon slices (about 4 ounces total), cut into 1-inch pieces

2   tablespoons olive oil

1½ cups chopped leeks, white and light green parts only (about 2 medium leeks)

1   tablespoon minced garlic

5   cups chicken stock, preferably Made-from-Scratch Chicken Stock (page 16) or Shortcut Chicken Stock (page 20)

4   cups coarsely chopped Savoy cabbage (from 1 medium head)

4   ounces snow peas, ends trimmed, cut into ½-inch-thick pieces on the diagonal

1   bunch green onions, including 2 inches of green tops, cut on the diagonal into ½-inch-thick slices

Kosher salt

2   tablespoons chopped fresh flat-leaf parsley

1. Sauté bacon pieces until golden and crisp in a medium, heavy pot set over medium heat. Using slotted spoon, transfer bacon to paper towels to drain. Remove and discard drippings in pan.

2. Return pan to medium heat and add the olive oil. When hot, add the leeks and sauté, stirring, until softened, for about 3 minutes. Add garlic and cook, stirring, for 1 minute more. (Soup can be made to this point 1 day ahead; cool, cover and refrigerate. Reheat, stirring, over medium-low heat.)

3. Add stock and bring mixture to a simmer. Add cabbage, snow peas, and green onions and cook until cabbage has wilted and snow peas and green onions are crisp-tender, for about 3 minutes.

4. Taste soup and season with salt, as needed. To serve, ladle soup into 4 bowls and garnish each serving with bacon and parsley. Serve immediately.

Emily's Springtime Salmon Chowder

My assistant, Emily Bell, loves chowders and created this one to welcome spring. As befits the season, it is lighter in texture than most chowders because no flour is used. What delights the palate in this version is the harmonious combination of ingredients: diced Yukon gold potatoes, sliced pencil-thin asparagus spears, slivers of green onions, and bits of coral-hued salmon—all accented by a trio of spring herbs.

SERVINGS: 4

PREP TIME:
15 minutes

START TO FINISH:
30 to 40 minutes

MAKE AHEAD:
No

BREAD BASKET CHOICE:
Crusty peasant loaf or sourdough

SOUP-ER SIDE:
Watercress Salad with Red Onion and Chopped Egg Vinaigrette (page 146)

1 ½ tablespoons unsalted butter

1   pound Yukon gold potatoes, unpeeled, scrubbed, cut into ½-inch cubes

¼   cup finely chopped sweet onion, such as Vidalia

½   teaspoon minced garlic

3   cups chicken stock

1   bunch green onions, including 2 inches of green tops, cut on the diagonal into ¼-inch-thick slices

4   ounces thin asparagus, tough bases snapped off and discarded, tips removed and reserved, and stalks cut on the diagonal into 1-inch-thick pieces

½   cup half-and-half

One 8-ounce piece skinless salmon fillet, skinned and cut into ¾-inch cubes

Kosher salt

Freshly ground black pepper

2   teaspoons chopped fresh mint

2   teaspoon chopped fresh chives

2   teaspoons chopped fresh dill

1. Heat butter in a large, heavy saucepan (with a lid) set over medium heat. When hot, add the cubed potatoes and cook, stirring often, for 5 minutes. Add the onion and cook, stirring constantly, for 2 minutes more. Stir in the garlic, reduce heat to low, and cover pot. Cook for 2 minutes. Mash the potatoes in the pot with the back of a fork.

2. Add chicken stock to potatoes and increase heat to medium. Stir well to scrape up the brown bits on the bottom of the pan. Bring mixture to a simmer and add the green onions and sliced asparagus (reserving the tips). Cover, reduce heat, and simmer until the asparagus stalks are just tender, for about 3 minutes. Stir in the half-and-half, reserved asparagus tips, and the salmon. Turn off heat and cover. The salmon will be opaque and cooked through in 3 to 4 minutes. Taste chowder and season with salt, as needed, and several grinds of pepper.

3. To serve, ladle soup into 4 bowls and garnish each serving with a sprinkle of chopped mint, chives, and dill. Serve immediately.

COOKING TIP:

If you like, you can add ½ cup of snow peas to the chowder. Trim the ends and cut the peas on the diagonal into 1-inch-thick pieces. Add them to the soup when you add the salmon.

Sweet Pea Soup with Early Chives

This soup does not take much time to prepare and holds up well when made a day in advance. It is light and delicate in taste (not rich and filling like its winter counterpart, split pea soup) and could easily begin a spring dinner. Although fresh peas would be my first choice, frozen ones will also work quite nicely.

SERVINGS: 6

PREP TIME:
10 minutes

START TO FINISH:
45 minutes

MAKE AHEAD:
Yes

BREAD BASKET CHOICE:
Crusty baguette, country peasant loaf, or sourdough

SOUP-ER SIDE:
Green Bean, Cherry Tomato, and Bacon Salad (page 143), or omit bread and serve with Crab and Avocado Sandwiches (page 155)

1 ½ tablespoons unsalted butter

2 cups chopped leeks, white and light green parts only (about 3 medium leeks)

5 cups fresh peas or frozen thawed peas, patted dry (see note)

1 medium Yukon gold potato (about 8 ounces), peeled and cut into ½-inch cubes

1 teaspoon kosher salt, plus more if needed

5 ½ cups chicken stock

¾ cup sour cream, divided

¼ teaspoon freshly ground nutmeg

⅛ to ¼ teaspoon cayenne pepper

1 ½ tablespoons chopped fresh chives

 AT THE MARKET NOTE:

Two and a half 10-ounce packages of frozen peas will yield approximately 5 cups. One pound of peas in the pod will yield about 1 cup shelled peas.

COOKING TIP:

Freshly ground nutmeg has a better and more pronounced flavor (it's more pungent and sweetly aromatic) than the powdered variety. Buy whole nutmegs, which can be found packaged in jars in the supermarket spice section, and scrape against a spice grater or the smallest holes of a box grater when needed. Store the remaining nutmeg in a closed spice jar.

1. Heat butter in a medium pot over medium-high heat. When hot, add leeks and sauté, stirring until softened, for about 4 minutes. Add peas, potatoes, and 1 teaspoon salt. Cook and stir a few seconds more. Add stock and bring mixture to a simmer. Reduce heat and cook at a gentle simmer until vegetables are very tender, for 15 to 20 minutes.

2. Purée the soup in batches in a food processor, blender, or food mill, and return soup to the pot. (Or use an immersion blender to purée the soup in the pot.) Whisk in ½ cup sour cream. Then whisk in the nutmeg and cayenne pepper. (Use ⅛ teaspoon cayenne for a milder taste, ¼ teaspoon for more heat.) Taste soup and season with salt, as needed. (Soup can be made 1 day ahead; cool, cover and refrigerate. Reheat, stirring, over medium-low heat.)

3. To serve, ladle soup into 6 soup bowls and garnish the center of each serving with a dollop of the remaining ¼ cup sour cream and a sprinkle of chives.

Watercress Soup with Pan-Seared Scallops

While touring through England's beautiful Cotswolds several years ago, I had an especially memorable dish at one of the area's many fine restaurants: a creamy, light green watercress soup topped with a single sautéed sea scallop. I knew from my first sip that this creation was a winner. Once I had returned to this side of the Atlantic, I worked out a close facsimile.

SERVINGS: 6

PREP TIME:
10 minutes

START TO FINISH:
1 hour

MAKE AHEAD:
Partially

BREAD BASKET CHOICE:
Crusty peasant loaf, sourdough, or ciabatta

SOUP-ER SIDE:
Best-Ever Greens Salad in Classic Vinaigrette (page 139), made with mixed greens and sliced radishes

3 ½ tablespoons unsalted butter, divided

3 cups chopped leeks, white and light green parts only (4 to 5 medium leeks)

2 medium russet potatoes, peeled and cut into 1-inch cubes (about 3 cups)

4 ½ cups chicken stock

2 ¼ cups trimmed and coarsely chopped watercress, plus 6 attractive sprigs for the garnish (from 2 large bunches)

½ cup sour cream

¾ cup whole milk

1 teaspoon kosher salt, plus more if needed

Freshly ground black pepper

1 tablespoon vegetable oil

6 jumbo sea scallops, side muscles removed

1. Melt 2 ½ tablespoons butter in a heavy, large saucepan over medium-high heat. Add leeks and potatoes, and sauté until leeks are tender, for about 4 minutes. Add stock and bring to a simmer. Reduce heat to medium-low. Cover and simmer until potatoes are tender, stirring occasionally, for about 20 minutes. Remove from heat and add chopped watercress. Cover; let stand until watercress wilts, for about 5 minutes.

2. Purée soup in batches in a food processor, blender, or food mill, and return soup to the pot. (Or use an immersion blender to purée the soup in the pot.) Whisk in sour cream. Thin soup with milk to desired consistency. (You may not need to use all the milk.) Season with 1 teaspoon salt or more, as needed, and pepper. (Soup can be prepared 1 day ahead. Cool, cover, and refrigerate. Reheat over low heat; do not let soup come to a boil.)

3. Melt remaining 1 tablespoon butter with oil in large skillet over medium-high heat. When hot, add scallops to skillet and cook until golden brown and just cooked through, for about 2 minutes per side. Season scallops with salt and pepper.

4. To serve, ladle soup into 6 shallow soup bowls. Place 1 scallop atop soup in each bowl, and garnish with watercress sprigs.

Paella Soup

I love to take traditional recipes and give them new twists. This one is a riff on the classic Spanish dish of saffron-hued rice studded with sausage and seafood. Once I came up with the idea, many failed attempts ensued until one day I found the right combination of techniques and ingredients. I combined sautéed onions, carrot, and celery with a little rice, seasoned the mixture with crushed saffron, and simmered it in stock and white wine. When puréed and enriched with some cream, the texture became smooth and the color deep golden. Familiar paella ingredients—shrimp, chicken, chorizo, and peas—were added as finishing touches.

SERVINGS: 4

PREP TIME:
15 minutes

START TO FINISH:
45 minutes

MAKE AHEAD:
Partially

BREAD BASKET
CHOICE:
Crusty peasant loaf

SOUP-ER SIDE:
Best-Ever Greens Salad
in Classic Vinaigrette
(page 139), made with
mixed greens

2	tablespoons olive oil
1	cup chopped onion
½	cup chopped carrot
⅓	cup chopped celery
¼	cup long-grain white rice
¼	teaspoon saffron threads, crushed
½	cup dry white wine
4	cups chicken stock
1	teaspoon kosher salt, plus more if needed
½	cup heavy or whipping cream
1	pound large uncooked shrimp, shelled and deveined
3	ounces Spanish chorizo sausage, cut into thin rounds or diced (see note, page 102)
1	cup fresh peas or frozen peas, thawed
½	cup diced cooked chicken, preferably white meat (optional; see note, page 102)
2	teaspoons chopped fresh chives

1. Heat oil in a large, heavy saucepan set over medium heat. When hot, add onion, carrot, and celery, and sauté until softened, for 3 to 4 minutes.

2. Add rice, saffron, wine, and stock and bring to a simmer. Season with 1 teaspoon salt. Bring mixture to a simmer, then reduce heat. Cover and cook at a simmer until vegetables and rice are soft, for about 20 minutes. Remove from heat and let cool for 10 minutes.

3. Purée the soup in batches in a food processor, blender, or food mill, and return soup to the pot. (Or use an immersion blender to purée the soup in the pot.) Stir in the cream. (Soup can be prepared to this point 1 day ahead; cool, cover, and refrigerate.)

continued on next page...

…continued

1. Set soup over low heat and, when mixture comes to a simmer, add shrimp, chorizo, peas, and, if desired, chicken. Cook until shrimp have turned pink and curled, for about 3 minutes. Do not overcook or shrimp will become tough. Taste soup and season with salt, as needed.

5. To serve, ladle soup into 4 bowls and garnish with a sprinkle of chives.

 AT THE MARKET NOTES:

For a convenient time-saver, purchase a roast chicken from the deli section of the supermarket.

Chorizo is a highly seasoned pork sausage available in both Spanish and Mexican varieties. For this recipe use the firmer, smoked Spanish type, which is made with pork that is already cooked. (Mexican chorizo is prepared with fresh pork enclosed in a casing.) Chorizo is available at Spanish markets, specialty food stores, and some supermarkets, such as Whole Foods.

Penne, Asparagus, and Peas in Parmesan Broth

Like the Primavera Vegetable Soup in a Lemon Broth on page 89, the key to this soup is using a high-quality stock. It calls for making a special batch of the Shortcut Chicken Stock with one additional ingredient: Parmesan cheese rinds are simmered along with the vegetables and herbs in the stock. (In Italian cooking, Parmesan rinds are commonly used to infuse rich flavor into vegetarian soups, such as minestrone.) You can make the stock ahead, then, at serving time, simply simmer the penne pasta, asparagus, and peas in the flavorful broth.

SERVINGS: 6

PREP TIME:
35 minutes

START TO FINISH:
45 minutes

MAKE AHEAD:
Partially

BREAD BASKET CHOICE:
Grissini (Italian bread sticks) or ciabatta

SOUP-ER SIDE:
Best-Ever Greens Salad in Classic Vinaigrette (page 139), made with arugula

8   cups Shortcut Chicken Stock (page 20)

8   ounces Parmesan cheese rinds, preferably Parmigiano-Reggiano, cut into 1- to 2-inch squares, plus 1/3 cup grated Parmesan cheese (see tip, facing page)

2   teaspoons olive oil

4   thin slices (about 2 ounces) prosciutto, cut into strips about 4 inches long by 1/4-inch wide

2   cups (about 5 ounces) penne pasta

1   pound medium asparagus, tough ends snapped off and discarded and spears cut into 1-inch-thick pieces

1   bunch green onions, including 2 inches of green tops, cut into 1-inch-thick pieces

1   cup fresh peas or frozen peas, thawed

Kosher salt

Freshly ground black pepper

2   tablespoons chopped fresh flat-leaf parsley

1. Prepare the Shortcut Chicken Stock according to the directions on page 20, adding the Parmesan cheese rinds to simmer along with the vegetables and herbs. Strain and reserve stock, discarding vegetables, herbs, and rinds. (The Parmesan stock can be prepared 1 day ahead; cool, cover, and refrigerate.)

2. Heat olive oil in a small, heavy skillet over medium heat. When hot, add prosciutto and cook, stirring, until crisp, for 4 to 5 minutes. Set aside. (Prosciutto can be sautéed 2 hours ahead; leave at cool room temperature.)

3. When ready to cook and serve soup, place the stock in a large, heavy saucepan or pot set over medium heat and bring to a simmer. Add penne and cook for about 9 minutes (or 3 minutes less than the package directions). Add asparagus and cook for 2 minutes, then add green onions and peas and cook for 2 minutes more. Taste soup and season with salt, as needed, and with 4 to 5 grinds of pepper.

4. To serve, ladle soup into 6 shallow soup bowls and garnish each serving with some crispy prosciutto, grated Parmesan, and chopped parsley. Serve immediately.

COOKING TIP:

This recipe offers a practical way to use up Parmesan cheese rinds. I always have several on hand in my fridge, but have noticed that the cheese departments of some supermarkets also sell the rinds separately. When simmered in broth, the rinds add an extra depth of flavor. However, if you don't have any, you can make this soup without them; just increase slightly the grated Parmesan you add as a garnish.

PHOTO ON RIGHT:
Grissini (Italian bread sticks)

Thai-Style Lemongrass Soup with Shrimp

This low-in-fat, high-in-flavor soup is made by infusing simmering chicken stock with chopped lemongrass and lime slices. The broth is strained, then a colorful array of vegetables and shrimp is added to the pot and quickly cooked. With its hint of citrus, this soup is light and refreshing, but, served piping hot, it will satisfy even the hungriest diners.

SERVINGS: 4

PREP TIME:
20 minutes

START TO FINISH:
25 to 30 minutes

MAKE AHEAD:
Partially

BREAD BASKET CHOICE:
Southeast Asian soups are typically served without bread.

SOUP-ER SIDE:
Red, Yellow, and Orange Pepper Salad with Tequila-Lime Dressing (page 148); omit the tequila in the dressing and serve the salad with an additional garnish of ½ cup coarsely chopped salted peanuts.

3	lemongrass stalks (see note)
2	limes
4	cups low-sodium chicken broth
8	ounces thinly sliced mushrooms
1	large red bell pepper, seeds and membranes removed, cut into ½-inch-thick pieces
½	teaspoon red pepper flakes
1	pound large uncooked shrimp, shelled and deveined
1	cup (3½ to 4 ounces) snow peas, ends trimmed, cut on diagonal into ½-inch-thick slices
2	green onions, including 2 inches of green tops, thinly sliced
1	teaspoon kosher salt, plus more if needed
3	tablespoons chopped fresh cilantro

AT THE MARKET NOTE:

Lemongrass, a long, slightly woody, grayish-green stalk about the size of a green onion, can be found in the produce section of many supermarkets and in Asian markets. Its slightly sour-lemon taste is an important ingredient in Thai and Vietnamese cooking. Store it in a plastic bag for up to 2 weeks in the refrigerator.

1. Remove the tough outer layers from the lemongrass stalks and discard them. Cut off and discard about 1 inch of the woody base from each stalk. Starting at the bases and cutting up to where the leaves begin to branch, thinly slice stalks crosswise to yield ⅓ cup.

2. Cut 6 thin slices from one of the limes and juice remaining limes to yield 2 tablespoons.

3. In a large nonreactive saucepan, combine chicken broth, sliced lemongrass, and lime slices. Bring mixture to a simmer over medium heat and simmer gently for 10 minutes to flavor the stock. Strain stock, discarding lemongrass and lime. (The stock can be prepared 1 day ahead; cool, cover, and refrigerate. Reheat over medium heat. Cover and chill the squeezed lime juice separately.)

4. Return the strained stock to saucepan set over medium heat. Add the mushrooms, red bell pepper, and red pepper flakes. Simmer for 5 minutes. Add shrimp, snow peas, and green onions. Cook until shrimp are curled and pink, for 2 to 3 minutes. Do not overcook or shrimp will become tough.

5. Remove from heat and stir in 2 tablespoons lime juice. Season with 1 teaspoon salt, or to taste.

6. To serve, ladle soup into 4 soup bowls and garnish each serving with a generous sprinkling of cilantro.

Corned Beef and Cabbage Soup—"Under Cover"

Perfect to serve on St. Patrick's or on any chilly spring day, this delicious soup stars corned beef, cabbage, and potatoes—that popular trinity used in Irish cooking. These ingredients are simmered in chicken stock along with seasonings of bacon and country Dijon mustard, then the soup is ladled into ramekins, covered with rounds of purchased puff pastry, and baked. At the table, this soup delights diners. They break into the golden, flaky pastry with a spoon and discover the savory mixture bubbling beneath. Plan one day ahead before serving this soup: the frozen puff pastry needs to thaw in the refrigerator overnight before using.

SERVINGS: 8

PREP TIME:
25 minutes

START TO FINISH:
2 ½ hours

MAKE AHEAD:
Yes

BREAD BASKET CHOICE:
You don't need to offer bread with this soup because it has pastry on top.

SOUP-ER SIDE:
Best-Ever Greens Salad in Classic Vinaigrette (page 139), made with watercress

5   bacon slices, cut crosswise into ¼-inch-thick pieces

1 ¼ cups chopped onion

1   small (1 ½ pounds) green cabbage, quartered and cored, cut into strips 2-inches long by ½-inch wide

1 ½ pounds russet potatoes, peeled and cut into ⅜-inch cubes

5   cups chicken stock

2   tablespoons whole-grain Dijon mustard

8   ounces sliced good-quality corned beef, cut into strips 2-inches long by ½-inch wide (see note)

Kosher salt

1   teaspoon freshly ground black pepper

One 17.3-ounce package frozen puff pastry, thawed overnight in the refrigerator

1   large egg

EQUIPMENT NEEDED:
Eight 1-cup ramekins or soufflé dishes

1. In a large, heavy pot (with a lid) set over medium heat, sauté the bacon until crisp. Add the onion and sauté with the bacon until onion is just slightly softened, for about 2 minutes. Add the cabbage and potatoes and toss to coat with the bacon drippings. Cover, reduce heat to low, and cook for 3 minutes.

2. Add the stock and the mustard to the pot and stir to blend. Bring the mixture to a gentle simmer, then cover. Simmer until vegetables are just tender, for about 20 minutes. Stir in the corned beef, and season with salt, as needed, and with 1 teaspoon pepper.

3. While soup is simmering, prepare pastry tops. On a floured work surface, roll one of the pastry sheets into an 11-inch square. Cut out 4 pastry rounds, each about 5 ½ inches in diameter (or ½ inch wider all around than the tops of the ramekins). Repeat with remaining pastry sheet. Cut a ½-inch circle in the center of each pastry round (a plain ½-inch pastry tip works well for cutting the hole). The hole will let the steam escape while the pastry bakes. Cover and refrigerate rounds until needed.

continued on next page…

...continued

4. When soup is done, let cool slightly, for about 10 minutes. Fill each ramekin with soup to within ½ inch of the top. (You will have about 2 cups soup remaining; refrigerate and enjoy as leftovers.) Whisk the egg with 1 teaspoon cold water in a small bowl, and brush one side of each pastry circle with some of the egg mixture. Carefully place a pastry round, glazed side down, over each ramekin. Firmly press the overlapping pastry against the outside of each ramekin. Be careful not to press down from the top to avoid cutting the dough on the edge of the ramekin. Press the tines of a fork around the pastry sides to make it adhere tightly to each ramekin.

5. Brush the tops and sides of pastry with the egg glaze. Place ramekins on a baking sheet and refrigerate, loosely covered with plastic wrap, for at least 1 hour. (Soup can be prepared 4 hours ahead; keep covered and refrigerated.)

6. To bake ramekins, arrange an oven rack at center position and preheat oven to 400 degrees F. Remove the plastic wrap and bake ramekins on baking sheet until pastry is golden brown and slightly puffed, for 18 to 20 minutes. Remove and serve.

 AT THE MARKET NOTE:

Be sure to buy the highest quality corned beef available, preferably from a deli or the deli counter at the supermarket. Don't be afraid to ask the salesperson for a taste of different corned beef brands—you might be surprised by how much they vary in flavor.

5

Summer

JUNE | JULY | AUGUST

There's no place I'd rather spend a summer Saturday morning than at the weekly farmers' market held in the center of our town common. There are bins filled with corn picked only a few hours earlier. Ditto the summer squash, cucumber crops, and so much more. Herbs are plentiful and inexpensive; melons are sweet and ready for slicing. And the summer tomatoes we wait for all year can be found in every color of the rainbow.

Many trips to this market have served as inspiration for the soups in this chapter. Fresh, sweet corn kernels from ears of summer corn are a mainstay. Here, they are used as the base for Creamy Corn Bisque with Crab and Fresh Basil. On one occasion, I was so taken with some beautiful snowy white cauliflower that had been harvested that very morning that I promptly bought a head, then rushed home to turn this vegetable—which I usually use in my winter cooking—into a chilled, velvety smooth soup topped with crisp bits of bacon and snipped fresh dill.

On the following pages, you'll find an array of chilled creations designed to help you beat the heat. Sips of Icy Cucumber Soup with Smoked Salmon and Dill or Zucchini Vichyssoise will cool you down even on the sultriest days. Two gazpachos, one a traditional Iberian production, the other a new version featuring watermelon, will also provide refreshing relief as the mercury rises. Shaker Summer Tomato, Celery, and Corn Chowder and Summer Squash Minestrone with Pistou are made with a bounty of vegetables and served warm—perfect for those cooler nights when evening breezes stir the air.

I love those familiar Gershwin lyrics: "Summertime, and the livin' is easy." For me, that is what summer soups are all about: easy living and eating well. Serve them for lunch or supper partnered with a salad or sandwich. Pour them into a thermos and head for a park or the beach, or make them a showstopping beginning to a backyard supper. These soups are easy to prepare, alive with color, and packed with fresh flavor.

Avocado Soup with Fresh Tomato Salsa

If you like guacamole, you'll love this soup. A smooth green purée of avocados is topped with a chunky, fresh tomato salsa. The salsa garnish is essential to the recipe; it makes the flavor of the avocados really shine.

SERVINGS: 6

PREP TIME:
20 minutes

START TO FINISH:
35 to 40 minutes, plus
3 hours for the soup
to chill

MAKE AHEAD:
Yes

**BREAD BASKET
CHOICE:**
Tortilla chips

SOUP-ER SIDE:
Red, Yellow, and
Orange Pepper Salad
with Tequila-Lime
Dressing (page 148)

SALSA

2   cups diced tomatoes (6 to 8 plum tomatoes, stems, seeds, and membranes removed and discarded, cut into ½-inch pieces)

1   cup finely chopped onion

1½ tablespoons minced jalapeño pepper (about one 3-inch pepper, with seeds and membranes discarded; see tip, page 22)

1½ tablespoons fresh lime juice

2   teaspoons grated lime zest (from 2 to 3 limes)

½   teaspoon kosher salt

¼   cup chopped cilantro

SOUP

2   tablespoons olive oil

1   cup chopped onion

1   tablespoon minced garlic

2   cups chicken stock

6   ripe medium avocados, peeled, pitted, and diced (reserve pits; see tip, page 114)

5   tablespoons fresh lime juice, plus more if needed

1   teaspoon kosher salt, plus more as needed

½   teaspoon Tabasco sauce, plus extra for the garnish

1. *To make salsa:* Combine tomatoes, onion, minced jalapeño, lime juice and zest, and ½ teaspoon salt in a medium nonreactive bowl. Toss to mix. (Salsa can be prepared 6 hours ahead. Cover and refrigerate.)

2. *To make soup:* Heat oil in a large, heavy nonreactive pot set over medium heat. Add onion and cook, stirring, until softened and translucent, for 3 to 4 minutes. Add garlic and cook, stirring, for 1 minute more. Add stock, 2 cups water, avocados, lime juice, 1 teaspoon salt, and ½ teaspoon Tabasco; bring mixture to a simmer and cook for 5 minutes. Remove from heat.

3. Purée the soup in batches in a food processor, blender, or food mill, and return soup to the pot. (Or use an immersion blender to purée the soup in the pot.) Don't worry if the soup is quite thick at this point. Add reserved avocado pits to soup, then cool, cover, and refrigerate for 3 hours or overnight. After soup has chilled, you can thin it with cold water, using up to 1 cup (or more if needed), if soup is too thick. Taste soup and season with more salt and additional lime juice, as needed. (Chilled soups often need extra seasoning to intensify their flavor.)

4. When ready to serve, remove and discard pits from soup. Drain the excess liquid from the salsa and stir in cilantro; season salsa with additional salt, if desired. To serve, ladle chilled soup into 6 bowls. Garnish center of each serving with some salsa and a dash of Tabasco.

continued on next page…

...continued

 COOKING TIPS:

The avocado pits come in handy in this recipe. When they are added to the puréed soup, they prevent it from turning a drab green.

See note about handling hot peppers on page 22.

PHOTO ON RIGHT:
Avocado

Chilled Broccoli-Mascarpone Soup

I love the simplicity and ease of this soup. Broccoli florets and chopped shallots are quickly cooked in chicken stock, then puréed. Creamy mascarpone is the secret ingredient in this recipe. It is whisked into the puréed soup while it is still warm, giving this potage its ethereally smooth texture.

SERVINGS: 8

PREP TIME:
10 minutes

START TO FINISH:
40 minutes, plus
3 hours for the soup
to chill

MAKE AHEAD:
Yes

BREAD BASKET
CHOICE:
Crusty baguette,
ciabatta, or a crusty
whole-grain loaf

SOUP-ER SIDE:
Green Bean, Cherry
Tomato, and Bacon
Salad (page 143) or
Best-Ever Greens in
Classic Vinaigrette
(page 139)

3　tablespoons olive oil

1½ cups sliced shallots (about 6 large shallots)

1½ pounds broccoli florets (see note)

6　cups chicken stock

1½ cups (12 ounces) mascarpone, divided

1　teaspoon kosher salt, plus more if needed

¼　teaspoon cayenne pepper, plus more if needed

3　tablespoons chopped fresh chives or
　　flat-leaf parsley

AT THE MARKET NOTE:

Packaged broccoli florets are a big time-saver; they are available in the produce section of most supermarkets.

1. Heat the oil until hot in a large, heavy pot (with a lid) set over medium heat. Add the shallots and sauté, stirring, until softened, for about 2 minutes. Add the broccoli and cook, stirring, 1 minute more. Add the stock and bring mixture to a simmer. Reduce heat to low, cover, and cook at a simmer until the vegetables are tender, for about 10 minutes. Let cool slightly for 10 to 15 minutes.

2. Purée the soup in batches in a food processor, blender, or food mill, and return soup to the pot. (Or use an immersion blender to purée the soup in the pot.) Reserve ¼ cup of the mascarpone for the garnish in a small bowl; cover and refrigerate.

3. With the soup off the heat, whisk remaining 1¼ cups mascarpone, a few tablespoons at a time, into the soup. Stir in 1 teaspoon salt and cayenne pepper. Let cool, then cover and refrigerate for 3 hours or overnight. When soup is well chilled, taste and season with more salt and cayenne pepper, as needed. (Chilled soups often need extra seasoning to intensify their flavor.)

4. Divide the soup among eight bowls. Garnish the center of each serving with a dollop of mascarpone and a sprinkle of chives or parsley.

Icy Cucumber Soup with Smoked Salmon and Dill

One summer when my husband and I were working in Paris and staying in an apartment without air conditioning, chilled soups were our respite from a dreadful heat wave. This cucumber creation was among our favorites. The lovely celadon green potage looks striking with rosy accents of salmon and snowy white swirls of crème fraîche.

SERVINGS: 6

PREP TIME:
35 minutes

START TO FINISH:
1½ hours, plus 4 hours
to chill soup

MAKE AHEAD:
Yes

BREAD BASKET
CHOICE:
Pumpernickel,
lightly toasted

SOUP-ER SIDE:
Watercress Salad
with Red Onion
and Chopped Egg
Vinaigrette (page 146)

1½ tablespoons unsalted butter

1   cup chopped onion

About 4 medium cucumbers, peeled, halved
    lengthwise, seeded, and cut into ½-inch-
    thick slices to make 5 cups

One 8-ounce russet potato, peeled and cut into
    ½-inch dice

3½ cups chicken stock

3   large dill sprigs, plus 6 tablespoons chopped
    fresh dill, divided

1   teaspoon kosher salt, plus more if needed

¾   cup crème fraîche, divided (page 23)

Freshly ground black pepper

2 to 3 teaspoons fresh lemon juice (optional)

2 to 3 ounces smoked salmon, cut into
    ½-inch pieces

1. Heat butter in large, heavy nonreactive pot (with a lid) over medium heat. When hot, add onion and sauté, stirring, until slightly softened, for about 3 minutes. Add cucumbers and diced potato and cook, stirring, for 1 minute more. Add stock, 3 dill sprigs, and 1 teaspoon salt. Bring mixture to a simmer, then reduce heat and cover. Simmer until cucumbers and potatoes are tender, for 25 to 30 minutes.

2. Purée the soup in batches in a food processor, blender, or food mill, and return soup to the pot. (Or use an immersion blender to purée the soup in the pot.) Let cool for 15 minutes, then whisk in ½ cup of the crème fraîche and 4 tablespoons of the chopped dill. Cool, cover, and refrigerate until soup is completely chilled, for about 4 hours or overnight. When the soup is well chilled, taste and season with salt and pepper, as needed. (Chilled soups often need extra seasoning to intensify their flavor.) If you would like a sharper flavor, season soup with 2 to 3 teaspoons lemon juice.

3. Divide soup among 6 shallow bowls. Sprinkle each serving with pieces of smoked salmon, garnish with a generous dollop of crème fraiche, and sprinkle with remaining chopped dill.

Victorine's Gazpacho

One of my favorite gazpacho recipes comes from my Portuguese friend, Victorine Fenandes, whose version of this classic Spanish soup is a true winner. The difference is in the details. She peels and seeds her tomatoes, and uses a French baguette instead of soft white bread, which adds more flavor and thickens the soup more efficiently. Her colorful garnishes also add to the allure. Victorine sets out a bowl of chopped red and green bell peppers mixed with chopped cucumber, another bowl filled with chopped hard-boiled egg and green onions, and finally, one with golden bread croutons sautéed in olive oil. This recipe serves 4 generously, but it can easily be doubled.

SERVINGS: 4

PREP TIME:
45 to 50 minutes

START TO FINISH:
1 hour, plus 1 hour or longer for the soup to chill

MAKE AHEAD:
Yes

BREAD BASKET CHOICE:
You don't need to offer bread with this soup since it is garnished with croutons.

SOUP-ER SIDE:
Crab and Avocado Sandwiches (page 155)

2	pounds tomatoes
1	large (about 8 ounces) red bell pepper
1	large (about 8 ounces) green bell pepper
1	cucumber
1	day-old French baguette with crust
3	garlic cloves, coarsely chopped
3	tablespoons olive oil, plus extra for sautéing cubed bread
1	tablespoon white wine vinegar
2	teaspoons sea salt, preferably fleur de sel (French sea salt), plus more if needed
8	ice cubes, crushed
2	hard-boiled eggs
1	bunch green onions

1. Bring a medium saucepan of water to a boil. Using a small, sharp knife, make an "x" on the bottom of each tomato, and add to the pan for 15 to 20 seconds. Remove with a slotted spoon. Using a small, sharp knife, peel skin from tomatoes and discard. Stem tomatoes, then quarter lengthwise and scrape out and discard seeds and membranes. Transfer tomatoes to a large bowl.

2. Stem the red and green peppers, then quarter lengthwise and cut out and discard seeds and membranes. Chop peppers and reserve ¼ cup of each for garnish. Add remaining chopped peppers to bowl with tomatoes.

3. Using a vegetable peeler, remove alternating lengthwise strips of skin from the cucumber. Quarter the cucumber lengthwise (but don't remove seeds). Chop the cucumber and reserve ½ cup for the garnish; add remaining chopped cucumber to the bowl of vegetables.

4. Cut the baguette into ½-inch cubes to yield 3 cups. Add half of bread cubes to the bowl of vegetables and reserve the other half for the garnish.

continued on next page

…continued

5. Add the garlic to the bowl of vegetables. Purée the vegetable mixture in two batches in a food processor or blender for several seconds; transfer to a large bowl. Stir in the olive oil, vinegar, and 2 teaspoons salt. Add the crushed ice. Taste and add more salt, as needed. Cover and refrigerate until icy cold, for at least 1 hour or up to 3 hours. After soup is well chilled, taste and season with salt, as needed. (Chilled soups often need extra seasoning to intensify their flavor.)

6. Set out 3 small bowls for garnishes. Mix reserved peppers and cucumber together and place in one small bowl. Cut off roots and all but 1-inch of green tops from green onions; chop onions. Chop the hard-boiled eggs and combine with onions; place in another small bowl. (These garnishes can be assembled 3 hours ahead; cover and refrigerate.)

7. Pour enough olive oil in a medium skillet to cover bottom generously. Set pan over medium-high heat. When hot, add the remaining 1½ cups bread cubes and cook, stirring, until golden, for 2 to 3 minutes. Remove and let cool, then transfer to remaining small bowl. (Croutons can be prepared 3 hours ahead. Store uncovered at room temperature.)

8. To serve, ladle soup into 4 large bowls. Arrange small bowls of garnishes on a tray and pass separately.

Watermelon Gazpacho with Grilled Watermelon Skewers

Gazpacho, that quintessential summer soup, comes in many colors and flavors. In addition to the traditional red-hued, tomato-based original, I've tried many variations. A few years ago in a small Parisian bistro, I sampled the most unusual creation so far—a watermelon gazpacho. A deep rose color, the soup was served icy cold, and was so enticing on a warm summer night that I asked the chef for the recipe. The following is my adaptation of the Parisian original.

SERVINGS: 6

PREP TIME:
25 to 30 minutes

START TO FINISH:
1 hour, plus 1½ hours
for the soup to freeze
slightly

MAKE AHEAD:
Yes

BREAD BASKET
CHOICE:
You don't need to offer
bread with this soup.

SOUP-ER SIDE:
Crab and Avocado
Sandwiches (page 155)

6   cups cubed watermelon, plus 12 extra
     1-inch cubes for garnish, seeded (from
     5-pound watermelon)

¾   cup bread crumbs made from a day-old
     French baguette with the crusts removed

2 ¼ teaspoons fresh lime juice, plus more
     if needed

¾   teaspoon kosher salt, plus more if needed

¼   teaspoon red pepper flakes

Olive oil for oiling the grill and for brushing on the
watermelon cubes

6   fresh mint leaves

EQUIPMENT NEEDED:

2   long skewers, preferably metal, for grilling
     (see tip)

6   short wooden skewers for the garnish

COOKING TIPS:

If using long wooden skewers, soak them for
30 minutes in water before grilling.

To chill water goblets or wine glasses, place them
in the freezer an hour before serving.

1. Place 6 cups cubed watermelon in a colander for 5 minutes to drain any excess liquid. Transfer ⅓ of the watermelon and ⅓ of the bread crumbs to a blender or food processor. Pulse mixture until slightly chunky and transfer to a large nonreactive bowl. Repeat with the remaining watermelon and bread in 2 more batches. Stir in the lime juice, ¾ teaspoon salt, and red pepper flakes.

2. Cover the bowl and freeze until mixture is slushy, but not frozen, for about 1½ hours or longer. Taste soup and season with salt and additional lime juice, as needed.

3. For the garnish, skewer the remaining 12 watermelon cubes on 2 long skewers and brush the cubes with olive oil. Oil a grill rack and prepare grill for a hot fire. Grill the watermelon, turning several times until grill marks appear, for about 5 minutes or longer. (You can also use a stovetop grill pan; oil the pan and place it over medium-high heat. Grill watermelon, turning until grill marks appear, for about 5 minutes.) Remove the watermelon from skewers and cool. (Watermelon can be grilled 1 hour ahead; leave at room temperature.)

4. Thread 2 grilled watermelon cubes with a mint leaf in between on each of the 6 short wooden skewers. To serve, ladle the icy watermelon gazpacho into 6 chilled water goblets or wine glasses, and garnish each serving with a watermelon skewer.

Chilled Carrot Soup with Cumin and Lime

When the thermometer is off the charts, nothing could be more tempting than this smooth, icy cold soup with slightly spicy accents. It's equally satisfying whether offered as a starter or as a light main course.

SERVINGS: 4

PREP TIME:
20 minutes

START TO FINISH:
1 hour, plus 3 hours for the soup to chill

MAKE AHEAD:
Yes

BREAD BASKET CHOICE:
Tortilla chips

SOUP-ER SIDE:
Red, Yellow, and Orange Pepper Salad with Tequila-Lime Dressing (page 148) or Crab and Avocado Sandwiches (page 155)

2 tablespoons olive oil

2 pounds carrots, peeled and chopped (about 5 cups)

2 cups chopped leeks, white and light green parts only (about 3 medium leeks)

1 tablespoon chopped garlic

3½ teaspoons ground cumin

½ teaspoon crushed red pepper flakes

6½ cups low-salt chicken stock, plus more if needed

8 tablespoons sour cream, divided

2 tablespoons fresh lime juice

Kosher salt

Freshly ground black pepper

2 tablespoons chopped fresh cilantro for garnish

2 teaspoons grated lime zest for garnish

1. Heat oil in a large, heavy pot over medium-high heat. Add carrots and leeks; sauté until leeks begin to soften but not brown, for about 5 minutes. Add garlic; sauté for 1 minute. Add cumin and crushed red pepper flakes; sauté for 30 seconds more. Add 6½ cups chicken stock. Bring to a boil; reduce heat and simmer uncovered until vegetables are very tender, for about 35 minutes.

2. Purée the soup in batches in a food processor, blender, or food mill, and return soup to the pot. (Or use an immersion blender to purée the soup in the pot.) Transfer soup to a large bowl and let cool, then whisk in 6 tablespoons of the sour cream. Cover and refrigerate for 3 hours or overnight.

3. When ready to serve, stir lime juice into soup. Thin soup with more stock, if desired, and season with salt and pepper to taste. (Chilled soups often need extra seasoning to intensify their flavor.) To serve, ladle soup into 4 bowls and spoon ½ tablespoon sour cream atop each serving. Sprinkle with cilantro and lime zest.

Cold Curry Creams

Several summers ago, on a warm, humid evening, I was seduced by an icy cold soup served at a dinner given by a friend. I noticed the deep golden color first, then I dipped my spoon into the bowl and swooned over the curried taste. I tried unsuccessfully to identify the other flavors, and finally asked my host to divulge the secrets. "Nothing fancy," she replied, explaining that she had simmered chicken stock with chopped onion and curry powder, then added bits of cream cheese and a touch of applesauce. After puréeing and chilling this mixture, she spooned a dollop of apricot jam into bowls, ladled in the soup, and sprinkled each serving with chives. The slightly hot curry was complemented by the sweetness of the applesauce and the jam, while the cream cheese contributed to the soup's velvety-smooth texture. You could serve this soup as the opener for a summer supper or pour it into a thermos and tuck it into a picnic basket.

SERVINGS: 6

PREP TIME:
20 minutes

START TO FINISH:
45 minutes, plus 3 hours
for the soup to chill

MAKE AHEAD:
Yes

**BREAD BASKET
CHOICE:** Grissini
(Italian bread sticks)

SOUP-ER SIDE:
Green Bean, Cherry
Tomato, and Bacon
Salad (page 143), or
omit bread and serve
with Vegetable Pitas
with Goat Cheese and
Fresh Herbs (page 152)

4	cups chicken stock
2	medium onions (12 ounces total), peeled and chopped
2	tablespoons curry powder
1	tablespoon cornstarch
8	ounces cream cheese, broken into small pieces
2	tablespoon applesauce
	Kosher salt
	Freshly ground black pepper
½	cup apricot jam or preserves
3	teaspoons chopped fresh chives

1. Put stock, chopped onions, curry powder, and cornstarch in a medium, heavy saucepan and whisk well to combine. Set saucepan over medium-high heat and bring to a simmer, whisking constantly. Cook, uncovered, until onions are softened, for 8 to 10 minutes. Remove from heat and stir in cream cheese and applesauce.

2. Purée the soup in batches in a food processor, blender, or food mill, and return soup to the pot. (Or use an immersion blender to purée the soup in the pot.) Strain soup through a large strainer into a large bowl. Let cool, cover, and refrigerate for 3 hours or overnight. When soup is well chilled, taste and season with salt and pepper, as needed. (Chilled soups often need extra seasoning to intensify their flavor.)

3. To serve, spoon a heaping tablespoon of apricot jam or preserves into 6 shallow soup bowls. Ladle soup over jam in each bowl. Garnish each serving with chopped chives.

Cold Cauliflower Soup with Bacon and Fresh Dill

This creamy, cold soup topped with bits of crispy bacon and chopped fresh dill is light enough to start a summer supper, yet satisfying enough to offer as an entrée. A hint of cayenne pepper adds a touch of heat to the soup, and a little cream provides the silken-smooth texture.

SERVINGS: 4

PREP TIME:
25 minutes

START TO FINISH:
1 hour 25 minutes, plus
3 hours for the soup
to chill

MAKE AHEAD:
Yes

**BREAD BASKET
CHOICE:**
Crusty baguette,
peasant loaf, or
sourdough

SOUP-ER SIDE:
Best-Ever Greens Salad
in Classic Vinaigrette
(page 139), or omit
bread and serve with
Vegetable Pitas with
Goat Cheese and Fresh
Herbs (page 152)

4   bacon slices

1½ cups chopped onion

6½ to 7 cups cauliflower florets (about
     1½ pounds cauliflower)

½   teaspoon kosher salt, plus more if needed

Scant ⅛ teaspoon cayenne pepper

3   tablespoons chopped fresh dill, divided

5   cups chicken stock

½   cup heavy or whipping cream

½   cup whole milk

1. In large, heavy deep-sided pot or saucepan set over medium heat, fry bacon until crisp. Transfer bacon to paper towels to drain. Reserve bacon for garnish. (Bacon can be fried 3 hours ahead; leave uncovered at room temperature.)

2. Pour off all but 1 tablespoon of drippings in pan and return to medium heat. Add onion and cook, stirring, until softened and lightly browned, for about 3 minutes. Add cauliflower, ½ teaspoon salt, cayenne pepper, 2 tablespoons chopped dill, and chicken stock. Bring mixture to simmer, then reduce heat, cover, and cook until cauliflower pieces are tender when pierced with knife, for 25 to 30 minutes. Purée the soup in batches in a food processor, blender, or food mill, and return soup to the pot. (Or use an immersion blender to purée the soup in the pot.)

3. Stir in cream and milk. Cool, cover, and refrigerate for 3 hours or overnight. When soup is well chilled, taste and season with more salt, as needed. (Chilled soups often need extra seasoning to intensify their flavor.)

4. When ready to serve, crumble reserved bacon. Ladle soup into 4 shallow soup bowls and sprinkle remaining 1 tablespoon chopped dill and the crumbled bacon over each serving.

"Cool and Hot" Tomato Chipotle Soup

Chipotle peppers are smoked jalapeños. They add a distinctive flavor to this simple tomato soup, giving it much more depth. Ground cumin provides a spicy accent, while garnishes of sour cream and chopped cilantro complement this deep red *sopa*.

SERVINGS: 6

PREP TIME:
30 minutes

START TO FINISH:
1½ hours, plus 3 hours
for the soup to chill

MAKE AHEAD:
Yes

**BREAD BASKET
CHOICE:**
Tortilla chips

SOUP-ER SIDE:
Red, Yellow, and Orange
Pepper Salad with
Tequila-Lime Dressing
(page 148), or Best-Ever
Greens Salad in Classic
Vinaigrette (page 139),
with some thinly sliced
avocado added

4   small dried chipotle peppers, about 3 to
    4 inches long (see note, facing page)

2½ to 2¾ pounds tomatoes

¼   cup olive oil

2¼ cups chopped onions

1   tablespoon minced garlic

2   cups low-sodium chicken stock

2   teaspoons kosher salt, plus more if needed

1¼ teaspoons ground cumin

⅓   cup sour cream for garnish

¼   cup chopped cilantro for garnish

1. Put the chipotle peppers in a bowl and cover with 3 cups boiling water. Soak peppers until softened, for 25 to 30 minutes. Remove peppers from water; using a fine-mesh sieve or a strainer lined with a paper towel, strain and reserve chipotle soaking liquid.

2. Halve chipotle peppers lengthwise and scrape out and discard all seeds. (The seeds are what make these peppers so hot; removing them will result in a spicy dish, rather than a fiery hot dish.) Finely chop the seeded peppers to yield 2 tablespoons; save any extra for another use.

3. Stem tomatoes and quarter them lengthwise. Scoop out and discard seeds and membranes. Cut tomatoes into ½-inch pieces to yield 5 cups.

4. Heat the olive oil in a large, deep-sided nonreactive pot over medium-high heat. When hot, add onions and cook, stirring, for 3 minutes. Add garlic and chopped chipotle peppers and cook, stirring, for 1 minute more. Add tomatoes, reserved

chipotle soaking liquid, chicken stock, 2 teaspoons salt, and cumin. Mix well and bring mixture to a simmer. Reduce heat to medium and cook, uncovered, until onions are tender, for 25 to 30 minutes.

5. Purée the soup in batches in a food processor, blender, or food mill, and return soup to the pot. (Or use an immersion blender to purée the soup in the pot.) Let cool, cover, and refrigerate for 3 hours or overnight. When soup is well chilled, taste and season with more salt, as needed. (Chilled soups often need extra seasoning to intensify their flavor.)

6. To serve, ladle soup into 6 soup bowls. Garnish the center of each portion with a dollop of sour cream and sprinkle with chopped cilantro.

 AT THE MARKET NOTE:

Chipotle peppers are sold both dried and canned in sauce. For this soup, I like to use dried chipotles, which are usually sold in cellophane packages in the produce section of many supermarkets. See note about handling hot peppers on page 22.

Chilled Melon Soup—Two Ways

Changing a single ingredient in the following recipe can produce two entirely different soups. One version calls for Pernod, the celebrated anise-scented French liqueur. It lends the soup a slight licorice taste, which pairs well with the sweetness of the melons. The other variation is accented with fresh lime juice, which adds a clear, bracing note to the fruit. Either one is a winner—it's your choice!

SERVINGS: 4

PREP TIME:
25 minutes

START TO FINISH:
1 hour 25 minutes, plus 3 hours for cubed melon to chill

MAKE AHEAD:
Yes

BREAD BASKET CHOICE:
You don't need to offer bread with this soup.

SOUP-ER SIDE:
Crab and Avocado Sandwiches (page 155)

½ cup sugar

1 cup torn fresh mint leaves, plus extra mint sprigs for garnish

4 teaspoons fresh lime juice, plus more as needed, or 4 teaspoons Pernod (see note)

4 cups cubed cantaloupe, cut into ½-inch dice (from 2 medium melons)

2 cups cubed honeydew melon, cut into ½-inch dice (from 1 large melon)

AT THE MARKET NOTE:
Pernod, an anise-scented liqueur, is available in stores where spirits are sold.

1. Combine sugar with 2 cups water in a heavy, medium saucepan set over medium-high heat. Stir until the sugar is dissolved. Bring to a boil, and boil for 5 minutes without stirring. Remove from the heat.

2. Put the torn mint leaves in a medium mixing bowl and pour the hot sugar mixture over them. Let the mixture steep for 45 minutes. Strain mixture into a large mixing bowl, pressing down firmly on the mint leaves to extract as much liquid as possible. Discard mint leaves. Stir in 4 teaspoons lime juice or Pernod.

3. Add the cubed cantaloupe and honeydew to the bowl and toss to coat. Cover bowl and refrigerate for at least 3 hours or overnight.

4. Strain 1½ cups cubed cantaloupe and honeydew melon from the mixture for the garnish. Purée the soup in batches in a food processor, blender, or food mill. For the lime version, taste the soup, and if you want a more pronounced citrus flavor, add 1 to 2 teaspoons additional lime juice (for the Pernod version, the liqueur will not need to be increased). Cover and refrigerate 3 hours or overnight.

5. To serve, ladle soup into 4 shallow bowls. Mound some of the reserved melon into the center of each serving and tuck in a mint sprig.

Zucchini Vichyssoise

Leeks and potatoes, that classic duo called for in traditional vichyssoise, are included in this recipe, along with zucchini. The latter blends in beautifully when simmered, then puréed, with the other ingredients, resulting in a soup with an attractive celadon hue. At the height of the zucchini season, when farmers' markets, groceries, and gardens are overrun with this squash, I was happy to discover a tempting new way to use this ubiquitous summer vegetable.

SERVINGS: 6

PREP TIME:
15 minutes

START TO FINISH:
1 hour, plus 2 hours for
the soup to chill

MAKE AHEAD:
Yes

**BREAD BASKET
CHOICE:**
Crusty baguette or
sourdough loaf

SOUP-ER SIDE:
Green Bean, Cherry
Tomato, and Bacon
Salad (page 143), or
omit bread and serve
with Vegetable Pitas
with Goat Cheese and
Fresh Herbs (page 152)

2   tablespoons olive oil

2 ½ cups chopped leeks, white and light green
     parts only (3 to 4 medium leeks)

1 ¼ pounds zucchini, ends trimmed and zucchini
     thinly sliced

1 ¼ pounds russet potatoes, peeled and cut into
     1-inch dice

4   cups chicken stock

1 ½ cups whole milk

1 ½ teaspoons kosher salt, plus more if needed

Freshly ground black pepper

½   cup plus 2 tablespoons sour cream, divided

3   tablespoons chopped chives

1. Heat oil until hot in a large, heavy deep-sided pot (with a lid) set over medium heat. Add leeks and cook, stirring, until softened, for 5 minutes. Add zucchini and potatoes and cook, stirring, 1 minute more. Add stock and bring mixture to a simmer. Reduce heat to low and cover. Cook until vegetables are soft, for 30 to 40 minutes.

2. Purée the soup in batches in a food processor, blender, or food mill, and return soup to the pot. (Or use an immersion blender to purée the soup in the pot.) Whisk in milk and season with 1½ teaspoons salt and several grinds of pepper. Cool, cover, and refrigerate for 3 hours or overnight. When soup is well chilled, taste and season with more salt, as needed. (Chilled soups often need extra seasoning to intensify their flavor.)

3. When ready to serve, whisk in ½ cup sour cream. Ladle soup into 6 bowls; garnish each portion with a dollop of the remaining 2 tablespoons sour cream and a sprinkling of chopped chives.

Shaker Summer Tomato, Celery, and Corn Chowder

My longtime assistant, Emily Bell, first had this soup in Pleasant Hill, Kentucky, a former Shaker community. While dining at the hotel restaurant there, she ordered this dish and loved its light taste and texture. The kitchen wouldn't divulge the recipe, so Emily returned home to create her own version. Perfect for summer, when fresh tomatoes and corn are in their prime, this warm soup is garnished with dollops of softly whipped cream and fresh chopped basil.

SERVINGS: 6

PREP TIME:
45 minutes

START TO FINISH:
1½ hours

MAKE AHEAD:
Partially

BREAD BASKET CHOICE:
Whole wheat or multi-grain loaf

SOUP-ER SIDE:
Best-Ever Greens Salad in Classic Vinaigrette (page 139)

3	tablespoons olive oil
2	cups chopped onion
2	cups chopped celery
1	tablespoon finely chopped garlic
6	cups diced plum tomatoes (4 to 4½ pounds plum tomatoes, stems, seeds, and membranes removed)
4	cups chicken stock, plus extra if needed
3	cups fresh corn kernels cut from the cob (from 5 to 6 ears of corn)
1 to 2	teaspoons kosher salt, plus more if needed
⅛	teaspoon cayenne pepper
1	cup heavy or whipping cream
2	tablespoons chopped fresh basil for garnish

1. Heat oil in a large, heavy pot set over medium to medium-low heat. When hot, add the onion and celery and sauté, stirring frequently, until transparent and tender, for 7 to 8 minutes. Remove ⅔ cup of this mixture and set aside.

2. Add the garlic to pot and sauté, stirring 1 minute more. Add the diced tomatoes and stock and bring mixture to a simmer. Cook until vegetables are tender, for 15 to 20 minutes. Let cool slightly.

3. Purée the soup in batches in a food processor, blender, or food mill, and return soup to the pot. (Or use an immersion blender to purée the soup in the pot.) Set the pot over medium-high heat and stir in the reserved onion-celery mixture and the corn kernels. Season the soup with 1 to 2 teaspoons salt and ⅛ teaspoon cayenne pepper. Bring to a simmer, then reduce heat and cook until corn is tender and flavors have melded, for about 15 minutes.

4. Stir ½ cup of the cream into the soup. Taste soup and season with more salt, as needed. (The soup can be prepared 1 day ahead. Cool, cover, and refrigerate. Reheat over medium heat.)

5. When ready to serve, whip the remaining ½ cup cream just until soft peaks form. Ladle soup into 6 bowls and place a generous dollop of the whipped cream (which will start to melt) atop each serving, then sprinkle with chopped basil.

Creamy Corn Bisque with Crab and Fresh Basil

It's hard to beat the delectable sweet flavor that fresh corn kernels provide in this bisque. At the height of the corn season, this is the soup to make. A generous accent of red pepper flakes adds a distinctive touch of heat to the slightly chunky mixture, while spoonfuls of fresh crabmeat and sprinkles of basil make tempting toppings.

SERVINGS: 4

PREP TIME:
20 to 25 minutes

START TO FINISH:
1 hour

MAKE AHEAD:
Yes

BREAD BASKET CHOICE:
Crusty baguette or sourdough loaf

SOUP-ER SIDE:
Green Bean, Cherry Tomato, and Bacon Salad (page 143) or Best-Ever Greens Salad in Classic Vinaigrette (page 139)

¼	cup olive oil
4	cups fresh corn kernels (from 6 to 7 large ears of corn)
2	cups chopped leeks, white and light green parts only (about 3 medium leeks)
1	tablespoon chopped garlic
1	teaspoon kosher salt, plus more if needed
¼	teaspoon red pepper flakes
4 to 4 ½ cups chicken stock
½	cup half-and-half
¼	cup sour cream
6	ounces fresh lump crabmeat, picked over
3	tablespoons finely julienned fresh basil, plus 4 to 6 basil sprigs for garnish

COOKING TIP:

This soup works beautifully as an appetizer. Ladle it into 8 espresso or demitasse cups and garnish with basil and crab.

1. Heat the olive oil until hot in a large, deep-sided pot (with a lid) set over medium heat. Add the corn and leeks, and cook, stirring constantly, until slightly softened, for about 6 minutes. Add the garlic, 1 teaspoon salt, and red pepper flakes and cook, stirring, for 1 minute more.

2. Add 4 cups of the stock and bring mixture to a simmer; reduce heat and cover. Cook at a gentle simmer until the corn and leeks are very tender, for 30 minutes.

3. Purée the soup in batches in a food processor, blender, or food mill, and return soup to the pot. (Or use an immersion blender to purée the soup in the pot.) The texture should be slightly chunky, not completely smooth.

4. Whisk the half-and-half into the soup, then whisk in the sour cream. Taste soup and season with salt, as needed. If the soup is too thick, thin it with up to ½ cup additional stock. (The soup can be prepared 2 days ahead. Cool, cover, and refrigerate. Reheat over medium heat. Do not let the soup come to a boil.)

5. To serve, ladle the soup into 4 soup bowls. Divide the crabmeat evenly and mound in the center of each serving. Garnish each portion with julienned basil and a basil sprig.

Coconut Lime Soup with Scallops

When the temperatures soar and you want to minimize your time in the kitchen, this soup comes to the rescue. It contains the hot-sweet-salty-sour flavors that are essential to Southeast Asian cuisines: coconut milk provides sweetness, fish sauce adds saltiness, red pepper flakes give it some heat, while lime juice and lemongrass are tart accents. Typically, chicken would be added to this soup, but I use scallops instead.

SERVINGS: 6

PREP TIME:
25 minutes

START TO FINISH:
50 minutes

MAKE AHEAD:
Partially

BREAD BASKET CHOICE:
Southeast Asian soups are typically served without bread.

SOUP-ER SIDE:
Red, Yellow, and Orange Pepper Salad with Tequila Lime Dressing (page 148); omit the tequila, and serve the salad with an additional garnish of ½ cup coarsely chopped salted peanuts.

---

3   stalks lemongrass (see note)

3   cups chicken stock

1   tablespoon minced fresh ginger

1½ cups coconut milk (see note)

1½ teaspoons Thai fish sauce (see note)

⅜   teaspoon red pepper flakes

1½ tablespoons fresh lime juice

12 ounces sea scallops, connective tissue removed and discarded

Kosher salt

3   teaspoons lime zest for garnish

¼   cup chopped fresh cilantro for garnish

1   lime, cut into 6 wedges for garnish

AT THE MARKET NOTES:

Lemongrass, a long, slightly woody, grayish-green stalk about the size of a green onion, can be found in the produce section of many supermarkets and at Asian and Thai markets. Its slightly sour-lemon taste is an important ingredient in Thai and Vietnamese cooking. Store it in a plastic bag in the refrigerator for up to 2 weeks.

Coconut milk and Thai fish sauce are available in the Asian foods section of many supermarkets. Thai Kitchen brand is widely available.

---

1. Remove the tough outer layers from the lemongrass stalks and discard them. Cut off and discard about an inch of the woody base from each stalk. Starting at the bases and cutting up to where the leaves begin to branch, thinly slice lemongrass crosswise to yield ¼ cup.

2. Combine the chicken stock, sliced lemongrass, and minced ginger in a medium, heavy saucepan set over medium-high heat. Bring to a simmer and cook for 5 minutes. Strain stock through fine-mesh strainer into large bowl; return broth to pan and discard contents of strainer.

3. Add coconut milk, fish sauce, red pepper flakes, and lime juice to pan and bring to a simmer. (Soup can be prepared to this point 4 hours ahead; cool, cover, and refrigerate. Reheat over medium heat before continuing.)

4. Slice each scallop horizontally into three rounds, then cut rounds in half to form half-moon shapes.

5. Add the scallops to soup and cook until opaque and cooked through, for 2 to 3 minutes. Taste soup and season with salt, as needed

6. Ladle soup into 6 bowls. Garnish each serving with ½ teaspoon lime zest and 2 teaspoons cilantro. Serve immediately with lime wedges to squeeze into soup.

Summer Squash Minestrone with Pistou

Lighter than its cold-weather counterpart, this summer minestrone makes a special centerpiece for a light lunch or supper during warm weather. Zucchini, yellow squash, and fresh tomatoes star in this version, rather than beans and hearty greens. Swirls of pistou—Provençal pesto—are added to bowls of the warm soup at serving time. You can easily double this recipe if you have a bumper crop of squash and tomatoes in your garden!

SERVINGS: 6

PREP TIME:
25 minutes

START TO FINISH:
45 minutes

MAKE AHEAD:
Partially

BREAD BASKET
CHOICE:
Ciabatta, focaccia, or
crusty peasant loaf

SOUP-ER SIDE:
Best-Ever Greens
Salad in Classic
Vinaigrette (page 139),
made with arugula

PISTOU

½ cup (loosely packed) torn basil leaves

1 teaspoon coarsely chopped garlic

6 tablespoons grated Parmesan cheese, preferably Parmigiano-Reggiano, plus some shavings for garnish (see tip, facing page)

3 tablespoons olive oil

SOUP

6 cups vegetable stock, preferably Made-from-Scratch Roasted Vegetable Stock (page 18)

¾ cup short pasta, such as tubetti, ditalini, or mini-penne

12 ounces tomatoes, stems, seeds, and membranes removed, cut into ½-inch pieces

1 cup thinly sliced red onion

Scant ¼ teaspoon cayenne pepper

1 pound small summer squash, preferably a mixture of yellow and green, thinly sliced (see tip, facing page)

Kosher salt

1. *To make the pistou:* Place the basil and garlic in a food processor fitted with a metal blade. Pulse until mixture is coarsely chopped. Add grated Parmesan; pulse until combined. With machine running, add olive oil in a thin, steady stream and pulse until the mixture is a smooth paste. (Pistou can be prepared 5 hours ahead; cover and refrigerate.)

2. *To make the soup:* Put the stock in a large, heavy saucepan set over medium heat and bring to a simmer. Add the pasta, tomatoes, onion, and cayenne; return mixture to a simmer and cook for 5 minutes. Add the squash and simmer for an additional 3 to 5 minutes, until pasta and squash are tender. Taste soup and season with salt, as needed.

3. To serve, ladle soup into 4 bowls; swirl 1 tablespoon pistou into each serving. Top each serving with shaved Parmesan, if desired. Serve immediately.

COOKING TIPS:

If you can't find small squash, halve or quarter larger ones lengthwise, then slice them.

To make Parmesan shavings, use a cheese slicer or vegetable peeler to shave thin strips from a 3- to 4-ounce piece of Parmesan cheese. (For best results, bring cheese to room temperature before making Parmesan shavings.)

PHOTO ON RIGHT:
Summer Squash

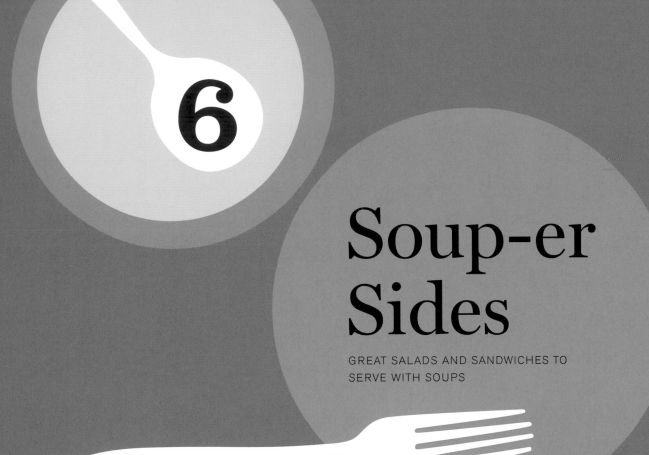

6

Soup-er Sides

GREAT SALADS AND SANDWICHES TO
SERVE WITH SOUPS

In this chapter, you'll find a dozen recipes for salads and sandwiches, each carefully chosen to complement the soups in this collection. The recipe for a basic green salad with classic vinaigrette is so simple and versatile that it works with almost every potage in this book. To serve with chilies and other spicy creations, you can try the Red, Yellow, and Orange Pepper Salad with Tequila-Lime Dressing. Italian soups like Ribollita or Spring Risotto Soup will pair well with an arugula salad tossed with lemon juice and Parmesan-infused olive oil.

The sandwiches are just as varied. You'll find warm ones, including a Turkey Panini with White Cheddar and Cranberry Chutney, and a Grilled Gorgonzola and Apple on Sourdough Bread to serve with robust inventions like Fabulous Fall Roots Soup. Some classics get a little updating: Crab and Avocado Sandwiches are made with a crab salad prepared with crème fraîche rather than mayonnaise, while Roast Beef and Watercress with Horseradish Cream sandwiches are extra special because of the vibrant yet light horseradish garnish bound with whipped cream. Try the crab and avocado duo with the Chilled Carrot Soup with Cumin and Lime and offer the roast beef combo with Tomato, Dill, and White Cheddar Soup.

Salads and sandwiches make ideal partners for soups. Start with my suggested pairings, but feel free to mix things up any way you like. After all, soups, salads, and sandwiches are always a winning combination!

Best-Ever Greens Salad in Classic Vinaigrette

Whenever I want to serve a really good, basic green salad, this is the recipe I follow. The vinaigrette takes no time at all to whip up, and if you buy greens that are already cleaned, you can count on about 10 to 15 minutes total to make the dressing and toss the greens in it. Choose whatever greens are in season for the best results.

SERVINGS: 4

PREP TIME:
5 to 10 minutes

START TO FINISH:
10 to 15 minutes

MAKE AHEAD:
Partially

VINAIGRETTE
2   tablespoons red wine vinegar
½   teaspoon Dijon mustard
½   teaspoon kosher salt
Freshly ground black pepper
⅓   cup olive oil

GREENS
5 to 6 cups salad greens, such as arugula, baby spinach, torn romaine, mesclun, or other greens of your choice
Kosher salt
Freshly ground black pepper
Red wine vinegar

1. *To make the vinaigrette:* Combine the vinegar, mustard, ½ teaspoon salt, and several grinds of pepper in a mixing bowl and whisk well to blend. Whisk in the olive oil. (The dressing can be made 2 days ahead; cover and refrigerate. Bring to room temperature and whisk well before using.) Makes about ⅓ cup.

2. *To assemble the salad:* Place the greens in a salad bowl, drizzle over about half the vinaigrette, and toss. Drizzle just enough of the remaining vinaigrette to coat the greens lightly. Taste and season with salt and pepper, as needed, and with a few drops of vinegar, if desired.

Arugula Salad Tossed with Parmesan Oil and Lemon

Arugula tossed in olive oil and lemon juice is a classic combination. In this version, however, the olive oil gets some extra flavor from being steeped with sliced Parmesan cheese. Set aside some time to make the Parmesan-infused oil and the cheese crumbles, then store them in the fridge to use when you like.

SERVINGS: 4

PREP TIME:
10 minutes, plus
2 hours for making
the Parmesan Oil
and Crumbles

START TO FINISH:
15 minutes, plus
2 hours for making
the Parmesan Oil
and Crumbles

MAKE AHEAD:
Partially

4 teaspoons fresh lemon juice, plus more
   if needed

½ teaspoon kosher salt, plus more if needed

Freshly ground black pepper

¼ cup Parmesan Oil (recipe follows) or olive oil

4 ounces (about 6 cups) arugula

Parmesan Crumbles (optional; recipe follows)

1. Combine the lemon juice, ½ teaspoon salt, and several grinds of pepper in a medium, nonreactive bowl. Whisk in the Parmesan Oil or olive oil. (The dressing can be made 2 days ahead; cover and refrigerate. Bring to room temperature and whisk well before using.)

2. Place arugula in a salad bowl and toss with enough dressing to just coat the leaves lightly. You may not need to use all the dressing. Taste and season with more salt and pepper, as needed, and with extra lemon juice, if desired. Mound arugula on 4 salad plates and, if desired, top with some Parmesan Crumbles.

Parmesan Oil and Parmesan Crumbles
MAKES ABOUT 1 CUP

One 4-ounce wedge Parmesan cheese, preferably Parmigiano-Reggiano

1 cup olive oil

1. Using a sharp knife, cut the cheese into 2-inch-square pieces that are about ¼-inch thick. Place the pieces in a small, heavy saucepan and cover with olive oil. Set pan over very low heat.

(It is important to keep the heat very low to prevent cheese from melting.) When oil just starts to gently bubble or simmer, cook for 10 minutes more at a very low simmer.

2. Remove pan from heat and let mixture stand at room temperature for 2 hours or longer, to allow the flavor of the cheese to infuse the oil. Remove cheese pieces and reserve. Occasionally, the cheese pieces will have stuck to the bottom and you will need to loosen them gently with a table knife. Strain the oil and cover and refrigerate until needed. (Oil will keep well for 1 week in the fridge. Bring to room temperature before using.)

3. Arrange reserved cheese pieces on a plate and let them dry out for 1 hour or longer. Using a sharp knife, coarsely chop cheese pieces. Save cheese crumbles to use as a garnish for salads or soups. Store crumbles in a resealable plastic bag in the refrigerator for up to 1 week. Bring to room temperature before using.

 AT THE MARKET NOTE:

Small, tender baby arugula (with its bite-size leaves) is particularly nice to use in this salad. If you can't find it, regular arugula leaves will work fine; just tear them into smaller pieces.

 COOKING TIP:

Although the Parmesan Oil and Parmesan Crumbles add extra flavor and interest to this salad, you can skip them if you're short on time. Instead, prepare the salad with good olive oil and use a vegetable peeler or cheese slicer to shave some Parmesan over the salad.

Green Bean, Cherry Tomato, and Bacon Salad

This salad was a big hit in one of my recent cooking classes. I listened with delight as student after student told me that they couldn't wait to go home and make this easy, colorful dish. A trio of simple ingredients—tender green beans, cherry tomatoes, and bacon—are tossed in a mustardy vinaigrette, then sprinkled with fresh snipped chives.

SERVINGS: 6

PREP TIME:
25 to 30 minutes

START TO FINISH:
45 to 50 minutes

MAKE AHEAD:
Partially

VINAIGRETTE

2 tablespoons red wine vinegar

¾ teaspoon Dijon mustard

¾ teaspoon kosher salt

Freshly ground black pepper

6 tablespoons olive oil

SALAD

1½ pounds tender green beans, trimmed and cut on diagonal into 2-inch pieces

9 to 10 bacon slices (about 8 to 9 ounces) cut into 1-inch pieces

1½ pints (12 ounces) grape or cherry tomatoes, halved lengthwise

Kosher salt

Freshly ground black pepper

3 tablespoons chopped fresh chives or flat-leaf parsley

1. *To make the vinaigrette:* Whisk together the vinegar, mustard, ¾ teaspoon salt, and several grinds of pepper in a small non-reactive bowl. Gradually whisk in the olive oil. (The vinaigrette can be made 2 days ahead; cover and refrigerate. Bring to room temperature and whisk well before using.)

2. *To make the salad:* Bring a large pot of salted water to a boil and add the beans. Cook until tender, for 6 to 8 minutes. Drain beans in a colander, and place under cold running water until beans are cold. Pat beans dry with a clean kitchen towel. (Beans can be prepared 6 hours ahead; place in a large resealable plastic bag and refrigerate. Bring to room temperature for 30 minutes before using.)

3. While the beans are cooking, set a large skillet over medium-high heat. Add bacon and fry in batches until browned and crisp. Using slotted spoon, transfer bacon to paper towels to drain.

4. Combine the beans, bacon, and tomatoes in a large bowl. Pour half the dressing over the ingredients and mix well. Add enough remaining dressing to coat well and toss to mix. (You may not need to use all the dressing.) Taste and season with more salt and pepper, as needed. Sprinkle with chives or parsley.

Roasted Pear, Walnut, and Feta Salad with Baby Greens

My talented assistant, Emily Bell, created this beautiful salad of golden roasted pears set atop a bed of baby romaine. The fruit and greens are tossed in a sweet-tart vinaigrette made with orange marmalade and balsamic vinegar, then topped with a sprinkling of toasted walnuts and crumbled feta.

SERVINGS: 4

PREP TIME:
15 minutes

START TO FINISH:
1 hour

MAKE AHEAD:
Partially

VINAIGRETTE

2   tablespoons balsamic vinegar
1   tablespoon sweet orange marmalade
1   tablespoon fresh orange juice
1   teaspoon whole-grain Dijon mustard
½   teaspoon kosher salt
Freshly ground black pepper
¼   cup olive oil

SALAD

1   tablespoon balsamic vinegar
1   tablespoon olive oil
4   medium red Anjou pears, slightly underripe
8   cups baby romaine or mixed baby greens
Kosher salt
Freshly ground black pepper
¼   cup coarsely chopped walnuts, toasted (see tip)
¼   cup crumbled feta cheese

1. *To make the vinaigrette:* Whisk together vinegar, marmalade, orange juice, mustard, ½ teaspoon salt, and several grinds of pepper in medium nonreactive bowl. Gradually whisk in olive oil. (The vinaigrette can be made 2 days ahead; cover and refrigerate. Bring to room temperature and whisk well before using.)

2. *To make the salad:* Arrange an oven rack at center position and preheat oven to 400 degrees F. In a small bowl, whisk together vinegar and olive oil. Halve pears lengthwise and core. Place pears in a shallow roasting pan and brush on all sides with the vinegar-oil mixture.

3. Roast pears, cut sides up, for 10 minutes. Turn pears over (cut sides down) and continue to roast until tender when pierced with a sharp knife, for 12 to 15 minutes more, depending on the ripeness of the fruit. The cut sides of the pears should be

browned and the skins slightly wrinkled when done. (Pears can be roasted 4 hours ahead; leave uncovered at room temperature. Reheat in the microwave for 1 to 2 minutes or in a preheated 350 degree F oven for 5 to 10 minutes until warm.) Cover pears with foil to keep warm while you assemble the salad.

4. Toss the greens with ¼ cup of the vinaigrette in a large bowl. Taste and season with more salt and pepper, as needed, and with a little extra dressing, if desired. Mound salad on 4 salad plates. Garnish each serving with two pear halves and sprinkle with 1 tablespoon each of walnuts and feta cheese. Drizzle some of the remaining dressing over the pears and salad on each plate. Serve immediately.

 COOKING TIP:

To toast walnuts, place on a rimmed baking sheet and bake in a preheated 350 degree F oven until lightly browned and fragrant, for about 7 minutes. Watch carefully to prevent burning. Remove from oven and let cool.

Watercress Salad with Red Onion and Chopped Egg Vinaigrette

What distinguishes this salad is its delicious dressing. Chopped hard-boiled egg, minced red onions, and chopped capers are added to a classic red wine vinaigrette. Peppery watercress sprigs are tossed in this mixture, then garnished with crisp, golden croutons.

SERVINGS: 4

PREP TIME:
35 minutes

START TO FINISH:
45 minutes

MAKE AHEAD:
Partially

VINAIGRETTE

2   tablespoons red wine vinegar

1   tablespoon coarsely chopped capers

½   teaspoon Dijon mustard

½   teaspoon kosher salt

Freshly ground black pepper

⅓   cup olive oil

⅓   cup chopped red onion

1   large hard-boiled egg, chopped

SALAD

3   tablespoons olive oil

1 ½ cups cubed good country-style or French bread with crust (½-inch cubes)

2   medium bunches watercress, tough stems removed and discarded

Kosher salt

Freshly ground black pepper

1. *To make the vinaigrette:* Mix together vinegar, capers, mustard, ½ teaspoon salt, and several grinds of pepper. Whisk in the olive oil. Add the chopped onion and chopped egg and stir just to mix. (The vinaigrette can be prepared 1 hour ahead; leave at room temperature.)

2. *To make the salad:* Heat the oil in a medium, heavy skillet over medium-high heat. When quite hot, add the bread cubes and cook, stirring, until crisp and golden, for 3 to 4 minutes. Remove and set aside. (Croutons can be prepared 1 hour ahead; leave uncovered at room temperature.)

3. To assemble the salad, put the watercress in a large bowl and toss with two-thirds of the dressing. Taste and season with salt, if needed. Divide salad among four salad plates and garnish each serving with some of the croutons. Drizzle the remaining salad dressing over the salads and grind some pepper over each. Serve immediately.

PHOTO:
Red Onions

Red, Yellow, and Orange Pepper Salad with Tequila-Lime Dressing

An unusual vinaigrette with a cool, refreshing taste makes this salad distinctive. I toss a trio of julienned sweet bell peppers with strips of romaine lettuce in it, and love the bright, crisp flavors provided by the lime and tequila.

SERVINGS: 4 to 5

PREP TIME:
15 minutes

START TO FINISH:
1 hour

MAKE AHEAD:
Partially

DRESSING

3	tablespoons olive oil
3	tablespoons fresh lime juice
1	teaspoon grated lime zest
1½	tablespoons tequila
¼	teaspoon kosher salt
¼	teaspoon red pepper flakes
1	garlic clove, smashed and peeled

SALAD

1	medium red bell pepper
1	medium yellow bell pepper
1	medium orange bell pepper
2½	cups sliced romaine lettuce (½-inch-wide strips cut from 1 large head)
2	teaspoons chopped fresh cilantro

Kosher salt

Freshly ground black pepper

1. *To make dressing:* Whisk together the olive oil, lime juice and zest, tequila, ¼ teaspoon salt, and red pepper flakes in a small nonreactive bowl. Add the smashed garlic clove. (Dressing can be prepared 1 day ahead; bring to room temperature before continuing.)

2. *To make salad:* Stem the peppers and halve them lengthwise. Remove and discard the seeds and membranes. Cut halves into ¼-inch-thick julienne strips. Put peppers in a large nonreactive bowl and toss with the dressing. Marinate for 30 minutes or up to 2 hours at room temperature.

3. When ready to serve, remove and discard the smashed garlic clove from the marinated peppers. Add the romaine and cilantro to the bowl and toss to combine. Season salad generously with salt and pepper.

Grilled Gorgonzola and Apple on Sourdough Bread

Crusty sourdough slices encase a filling of creamy blue cheese, chopped pecans, and sliced tart apples. Grilled until the bread is golden and crisp and the cheese has melted, these irresistible sandwiches make an especially good accompaniment to hearty soups.

SERVINGS: 4

PREP TIME:
20 minutes

START TO FINISH:
25 minutes

MAKE AHEAD:
No

½ Granny Smith apple, cored but unpeeled, very thinly sliced

½ teaspoon fresh lemon juice

8 crusty sourdough bread slices (⅜- to ½-inch thick)

8 ounces creamy blue cheese, such as Gorgonzola, Fourme d'Ambert, or Bleu d'Auvergne, thickly sliced

4 tablespoons chopped pecans

4 tablespoons unsalted butter, melted, plus more if needed

1. Toss apple slices with lemon juice in a medium nonreactive bowl.

2. For each sandwich, place about ¼ of the cheese on one slice of bread. Sprinkle with 1 tablespoon chopped pecans, and press down with your fingers. Add 3 to 4 apple slices, and cover with another bread slice. Brush both sides of the sandwich with a tablespoon or more of melted butter. Repeat to make 3 more sandwiches.

3. Place enough sandwiches to fit comfortably in a preheated stovetop grill pan, and press down on the top of each sandwich with a metal spatula. Cook until browned on underside, for about 2 minutes; turn, and continue cooking on the other side, pressing down with the spatula often, until browned and grill marks appear, for about 2 minutes.

4. Remove sandwiches from pan and cover loosely with foil; repeat until all sandwiches have been grilled. (If you don't have a grill pan, you can use a large, heavy skillet. Coat the bottom of the pan with a thin film of vegetable oil and heat until hot. Place sandwiches, which have been brushed with butter, in a single layer in skillet and cook as in a grill pan.)

5. Halve sandwiches on the diagonal and serve warm.

Roast Beef and Watercress with Horseradish Cream on Dark Bread

An easy-to-make, creamy horseradish sauce gives these sandwiches their spark. Softly whipped cream lightens the sauce, which is made from prepared horseradish, sour cream, and mustard. The sauce takes just minutes to put together, and it can be prepared several hours ahead. Watercress and red onions add more peppery accents to these out-of-the-ordinary roast beef sandwiches.

SERVINGS: 4

PREP TIME:
20 to 25 minutes

START TO FINISH:
25 to 30 minutes

MAKE AHEAD:
Partially

8 slices pumpernickel or rye bread
Horseradish Cream (recipe follows)
10 to 12 ounces thinly sliced roast beef
1 medium red onion, peeled and thinly sliced
1 bunch watercress
Kosher salt
Freshly ground black pepper

1. Spread one side of each bread slice generously with Horseradish Cream. Layer roast beef, some sliced onion, and several watercress sprigs on half of the slices. Season with salt and pepper, then top with remaining slices.

2. Halve sandwiches on the diagonal; place on a plate, and garnish with a few watercress sprigs.

Horseradish Cream
MAKES ABOUT 1⅔ CUPS

½ cup heavy cream
½ cup sour cream
¼ cup prepared horseradish (not horseradish sauce), drained, plus a little extra if desired
1 teaspoon Dijon mustard
1 teaspoon cider vinegar
¼ teaspoon kosher salt, plus more if needed
¼ teaspoon freshly ground black pepper, plus more if needed

1. Using an electric mixer, whip cream on medium-high speed until stiff peaks form. Set aside.

2. In a medium nonreactive bowl, whisk together sour cream, horseradish, mustard, vinegar, ¼ teaspoon salt, and ¼ teaspoon pepper. Gently fold in the whipped cream. Taste and add more salt and pepper, as needed. If you want a spicier sauce, add ½ to 1 teaspoon additional horseradish. Transfer mixture to a small bowl. (The sauce can be prepared 4 hours ahead; cover and refrigerate. Remove from the refrigerator for 10 minutes before using.)

Vegetable Pitas with Goat Cheese and Fresh Herbs

It takes some time to prep and roast the medley of vegetables used as the filling for these pita pockets, but they can be roasted several hours ahead so that all you need to do at serving time is toss them in an orange-scented dressing along with bits of goat cheese and slivered black olives. Although the following combination of vegetables is delectable, you can vary your choices according to taste and availability.

SERVINGS: 4

PREP TIME:
25 minutes

START TO FINISH:
1 hour 45 minutes

MAKE AHEAD:
Partially

VEGETABLES

1   medium red bell pepper

1   medium yellow bell pepper

1   medium zucchini

1   medium red onion (6 to 8 ounces)

1   medium fennel bulb

1   small eggplant (8 ounces) or half of a medium (1 pound) eggplant

6   tablespoons olive oil, plus more if needed

2   teaspoons kosher salt

2   teaspoons freshly ground black pepper

DRESSING AND GARNISH

1½ tablespoons red wine vinegar

1½ tablespoons fresh orange juice

1½ tablespoons olive oil

¾   teaspoon kosher salt, plus more if needed

½   teaspoon red pepper flakes

5 to 6 ounces creamy goat cheese, broken into small pieces

¼   cup pitted kalamata olives, slivered

½   cup fresh basil leaves torn into small pieces

Four 6-inch pitas, cut in half

1. Arrange oven racks at center and lower positions and preheat oven to 400 degrees F.

2. *To prepare the vegetables:* Halve peppers lengthwise and cut out and discard stems, membranes, and seeds. Cut each half into ½-inch-thick strips. Trim and discard ends from zucchini and cut into ½-inch-thick rounds. Halve onion lengthwise through the root ends, and then slice each half into ½-inch-thick wedges.

3. Cut off and discard stalks (if attached) from fennel. Halve the bulb lengthwise and cut out and discard the tough inner cores. Slice each half crosswise into ¼-inch-thick slices.

4. Halve eggplant lengthwise, and then cut each half crosswise into ½-inch-thick slices. (If using a medium eggplant, halve lengthwise and use only one half, cut into 1-inch cubes.)

5. Place vegetables in a large mixing bowl and toss with 6 tablespoons olive oil and the salt and pepper. Divide vegetables among 2 rimmed baking sheets and spread in a single layer.

6. Roast vegetables, stirring every 10 minutes, until tender and browned around the edges, for about 40 minutes. While roasting, if vegetables seem to be drying out, drizzle them with an additional 1 to 2 tablespoons olive oil. Remove from oven and let cool to room temperature. (Vegetables can be roasted 6 hours ahead. Cover loosely with foil and leave at room temperature.)

7. *To make the dressing:* Whisk together vinegar, orange juice, olive oil, ¾ teaspoon salt, and red pepper flakes in a small nonreactive bowl. (Dressing can be prepared 1 day ahead; cover and refrigerate. Bring to room temperature and whisk well before using.)

8. To serve, toss vegetables with dressing. Add goat cheese, olives, and basil and toss again. Season with more salt, as needed. Fill each pita half generously with vegetables.

Crab and Avocado Sandwiches

This sandwich was inspired by a distinctive crab-and-avocado salad I sampled at Oceana, a celebrated Manhattan seafood restaurant. I was stunned by the simple ingenuity of the dish. Typically, crab salad is mixed with mayonnaise and rarely includes a spicy accent, but this version was bound with crème fraîche and seasoned with cumin. At home, I made a close facsimile, and then mounded it on slices of toasted white bread. The recipe calls for a couple of tablespoons of crème fraîche, so you will have quite a bit left over. To get more use out of it, you might like to pair these sandwiches with a soup that calls for crème fraîche, like Tomato and Fennel Soup with Pernod Cream (page 60) or Heavenly Asparagus Soup with Tarragon Cream (page 87).

SERVINGS: 4

PREP TIME:
15 minutes

START TO FINISH:
30 to 35 minutes

MAKE AHEAD:
Partially

1	ripe (but not mushy) Hass avocado
8	ounces fresh lump crabmeat, picked over
¼	cup finely diced celery
¼	cup finely chopped green onion (about 4 green onions, including 2 inches of green tops)
2	tablespoons fresh lime juice
2	tablespoons crème fraîche (page 23)
1 ¼	teaspoons ground cumin
¾	teaspoon kosher salt, plus more if needed
¼	teaspoon dried red pepper flakes
8	slices good-quality white sandwich bread, lightly toasted

1. Halve the avocado lengthwise, and remove and discard the seed. Using a sharp knife, remove the flesh from both halves and cut into small dice. Place the diced avocado in a large nonreactive bowl; add the crab, celery, and green onion. Add lime juice, crème fraîche, cumin, ¾ teaspoon salt, and red pepper flakes to the bowl and toss gently to combine. Taste and season with more salt, as needed. (The crab mixture can be prepared 2 hours ahead. Cover and refrigerate. Bring to room temperature for 30 minutes before using.)

2. To serve, mound crab mixture on 4 toasted bread slices, then top with remaining toasted bread slices. Halve sandwiches on the diagonal and place on serving plates.

All-Time Favorite Egg Salad and Olive Sandwiches

Although I grew up eating egg salad sandwiches studded with pimiento-stuffed green olives, I've been surprised when friends have commented that it was an unexpected ingredient. The olives add a salty, slightly tart note that complements the eggs.

SERVINGS: 4

PREP TIME:
25 minutes

START TO FINISH:
35 minutes

MAKE AHEAD:
Partially

8   large hard-boiled eggs, peeled and coarsely chopped

¼   cup very finely chopped celery

3   tablespoons chopped Spanish olives (pimiento-stuffed green olives; see note)

¼   cup mayonnaise plus extra for spreading on toasted bread

½   teaspoon Dijon mustard, plus more if needed

½   teaspoon kosher salt, plus more if needed

¼   teaspoon freshly ground black pepper, plus more if needed

8   slices good-quality white sandwich bread, lightly toasted

8   slices lean bacon, fried until crisp and golden

8   crisp red leaf lettuce leaves

6-inch wooden skewers (optional)

AT THE MARKET NOTE:
Pimiento-stuffed green olives (rather than more exotic imported olives) taste best in this recipe.

1. Combine the eggs, celery, and olives in a large nonreactive mixing bowl. Stir in mayonnaise, mustard, ½ teaspoon salt, and ¼ teaspoon pepper, and mix well. Taste and season with more salt and pepper, if desired. (Egg salad can be prepared 4 hours ahead; cover and refrigerate.)

2. To assemble sandwiches, spread all toasted bread slices on one side very lightly with mayonnaise. Mound egg salad on 4 slices, break bacon slices in half and arrange 4 pieces over egg salad on each sandwich. Top with lettuce leaves and remaining toasted bread slices. Halve sandwiches on the diagonal with a serrated knife, and, if desired, secure halves with wooden skewers.

3. To serve, arrange 2 halves on each of 4 dinner plates.

Turkey Panini with White Cheddar and Cranberry Chutney

These sandwiches are easy to make, even if you don't own a panini-maker. I grill the panini on my stovetop grill pan, but they can also be toasted in a skillet. I like to use a crusty sourdough loaf, but any artisanal, rustic bread with a good crust will do.

MAKES: 4 sandwiches

PREP TIME:
10 minutes

START TO FINISH:
25 to 30 minutes

MAKE AHEAD:
No

Eight ⅜-inch-thick slices crusty sourdough or country-style bread slices

8 to 10 ounces sliced roast turkey

½ cup or more cranberry chutney (see note)

1 bunch watercress, cleaned and tough stems cut off and discarded

8 ounces thinly sliced sharp white Cheddar cheese, preferably a farmhouse Cheddar (see note)

Olive oil for brushing and grilling

 AT THE MARKET NOTES:

Cranberry chutney is available in specialty food stores and in some supermarkets, such as Whole Foods. If you can't find it, substitute whole cranberry sauce.

Farmhouse cheddar is an artisanally produced Cheddar cheese. Pale ivory in color, it has a rich, full flavor and a smooth, buttery texture. If not available, use good-quality sharp white Cheddar.

---

1. Place 4 bread slices on a work surface and top each slice with some sliced turkey. Spread 2 tablespoons or more cranberry chutney over the turkey and top with watercress sprigs. Cover the watercress with several thin slices of cheese. (There may be some remaining cheese slices.) Top with remaining bread slices. Brush the outside of sandwiches generously with oil.

2. If you have a panini machine, cook the sandwiches according to manufacturer's directions. Otherwise, brush a stovetop grill pan or skillet generously with oil and set over medium-high heat. When hot, place enough sandwiches in pan to fit comfortably in a single layer. Grill sandwiches, pressing down firmly with a metal spatula or with the bottom of a heavy skillet to compress the sandwiches. Cook until the undersides are golden brown, for about 2 minutes. Turn and cook until golden brown, for about 2 minutes more. Remove panini from pan, cover loosely with foil, and set aside. Repeat with remaining sandwiches, brushing pan with additional olive oil if necessary.

3. To serve, halve sandwiches on the diagonal; arrange on plates, garnished with some additional watercress.

Picking the Right Soup

Quick and Easy Soups (30 MINUTES OR LESS)

SPICY PORK CHILI WITH CUMIN POLENTA

Slow and Simmering Soups

"ABOUT 30 MINUTES" CHICKPEA AND PASTA SOUP WITH ROSEMARY

"All-in-One" Main Courses

Vegetables in Starring Roles

RIBOLLITA—THE TUSCAN MINESTRONE

COCONUT LIME SOUP WITH SCALLOPS

A Touch of Seafood

Lighter Fare with Big Flavors

FALL BRODO WITH ACORN SQUASH, SWISS CHARD, AND BACON

Soups for Holidays and Special Occasions

TOMATO AND FENNEL SOUP WITH PERNOD CREAM

Appetizer Soups
Serve mini-portions of these soups in espresso or demitasse cups

SPRING NEW POTATO AND GARLIC SOUP

Comforting Soups to Raise Your Spirits

HEAVENLY ASPARAGUS SOUP WITH TARRAGON CREAM

TABLE OF EQUIVALENTS

The exact equivalents in the following tables have been rounded for convenience.

LIQUID/DRY MEASUREMENTS

U.S	METRIC
¼ teaspoon	1.25 milliliters
½ teaspoon	2.5 milliliters
1 teaspoon	5 milliliters
1 tablespoon (3 teaspoons)	15 milliliters
1 fluid ounce (2 tablespoons)	30 milliliters
¼ cup	60 milliliters
⅓ cup	80 milliliters
½ cup	120 milliliters
1 cup	240 milliliters
1 pint (2 cups)	480 milliliters
1 quart (4 cups; 32 ounces)	960 milliliters
1 gallon (4 quarts)	3.84 liters
1 ounce (by weight)	28 grams
1 pound	448 grams
2.2 pounds	1 kilogram

LENGTHS

U.S.	METRIC
⅛ inch	3 millimeters
¼ inch	6 millimeters
½ inch	12 millimeters
1 inch	2.5 centimeters

OVEN TEMPERATURES

FAHRENHEIT	CELSIUS	GAS
250	120	½
275	140	1
300	150	2
325	160	3
350	180	4
375	190	5
400	200	6
425	220	7
450	230	8
475	240	9
500	260	10